STRATEGIC SKILLS FOR
PUBLIC HEALTH PRACTICE

SERIES

Policy Engagement

For access to digital chapters,
visit the APHA Press bookstore (www.apha.org).

Strategic Skills for Public Health Practice Series
Series Editors: Michael Fraser, PhD, MS, and Brian C. Castrucci, DrPH

1. *Systems and Strategic Thinking*
2. *Policy Engagement*
3. *Resource Management and Finance*
4. *Community Engagement*
5. *Advancing Equity and Justice*
6. *Effective Communication*
7. *Change Management*
8. *Data-Driven Decision Making*
9. *Cross-Sectoral Partnerships*

STRATEGIC SKILLS FOR
PUBLIC HEALTH PRACTICE

SERIES

Policy Engagement

Shelley Hearne, DrPH, MPH
Keshia M. Pollack Porter, PhD, MPH
Katrina S. Forrest, JD

American Public Health Association
800 I Street, NW
Washington, DC 20001-3710
www.apha.org

© 2023 by the American Public Health Association

All rights reserved. No part of this publication may be reproduced, stored in a retrieval system, or transmitted in any form or by any means, electronic, mechanical, photocopying, recording, scanning, or otherwise, except as permitted under Sections 107 and 108 of the 1976 United States Copyright Act, without either the prior written permission of the Publisher or authorization through payment of the appropriate per-copy fee to the Copyright Clearance Center [222 Rosewood Drive, Danvers, MA 01923, (978) 750-8400, fax (978) 646-8600, www.copyright.com]. Requests to the Publisher for permission should be addressed to the Permissions Department, American Public Health Association, 800 I Street, NW, Washington, DC 20001-3710; fax (202) 777-2531.

DISCLAIMER: Any discussion of medical or legal issues in this publication is being provided for informational purposes only. Nothing in this publication is intended to constitute medical or legal advice, and it should not be construed as such. This book is not intended to be and should not be used as a substitute for specific medical or legal advice, since medical and legal opinions may only be given in response to inquiries regarding specific factual situations. If medical or legal advice is desired by the reader of this book, a medical doctor or attorney should be consulted. The use of trade names and commercial sources in this book does not imply endorsement by the American Public Health Association. The views expressed in the publications of the American Public Health Association are those of the contributors and do not necessarily reflect the views of the American Public Health Association, or its staff, advisory panels, officers, or members of the Association's Executive Board. While the publisher and contributors have used their best efforts in preparing this book, they make no representations with respect to the accuracy or completeness of the content. The findings and conclusions in this book are those of the contributors and do not necessarily represent the official positions of the institutions with which they are affiliated.

Georges C. Benjamin, MD, MACP, Executive Director

Printed and bound in the United States of America
Book Production Editor: Maya Ribault
Typesetting: KnowledgeWorks Global, Ltd.
Cover Design: Alan Giarcanella
Printing and Binding: Sheridan Books

Library of Congress Cataloging-in-Publication Data

Names: Hearne, Shelley A., author. | Pollack Porter, Keshia M., author. | Forrest, Katrina S., author.
Title: Policy engagement / authors: Shelley Hearne, Keshia M. Pollack Porter, Katrina S. Forrest.
Description: Washington, DC : American Public Health Association, [2023] | Includes bibliographical references and index. | Summary: "This book aims to be a practical field guide to the unwritten rules, lessons, and insights needed to be a successful public health policymaker"-- Provided by publisher.
Identifiers: LCCN 2023012825 (print) | LCCN 2023012826 (ebook) | ISBN 9780875533384 (paperback) | ISBN 9780875533391 (adobe pdf)
Subjects: LCSH: Medical policy--United States. | Policy sciences--United States.
Classification: LCC RA395.A3 H4394 2023 (print) | LCC RA395.A3 (ebook) | DDC 362.10973--dc23/eng/20230601
LC record available at https://lccn.loc.gov/2023012825
LC ebook record available at https://lccn.loc.gov/2023012826

With enormous gratitude to all who inspire action and get things done.

Contents

Series Introduction		ix
Preface		xiii
Acknowledgements		xv
Introduction		1
1.	Policy Matters and So Do You	7
2.	A Look Into Where Policy Is Made	17
	Appendix 2A: US Department of Health and Human Services Operating Divisions	32
3.	Five Guiding Principles to Policy Engagement	35
4.	The Policymakers: What Do They Need to Make Good Public Health Decisions?	43
5.	It Has to Be Fair and Inclusive: Approaching Policy With Equity in Mind	55
6.	Leaning In: Selecting Your Policies and Ways to Engage	67
7.	Ready, Set, But Don't Go Alone	81
Appendix A: Organizations		87
Appendix B: Advocacy and Policy Change Resources		90
Appendix C: Abbreviations		92
About the Authors		95
Index		97

Strategic Skills for Public Health Practice Series Introduction

Over the last 15 years, governmental public health professionals and partners nationwide have worked to define core competencies, essential services, and foundational capabilities of the public health.[1,2,3] Central to all these efforts is the public health workforce—the practitioners who work in local, state, territorial, tribal, and federal public health agencies to prevent disease and protect and promote the health of the public.

The governmental public health workforce is diverse and comprised of many technical specialties and professions. These professional identities have shaped public health practice and formed categories of work that comprise the organizational chart most governmental public health agencies utilize, such as maternal and child health, environmental health, epidemiology and surveillance, communicable disease control, administration and finance, school health, and several others.

These categories have served public health well by helping organize work and allowing for professionalization and leadership development within specific areas. Over 21 national professional associations represent categorical or function areas within state and territorial health departments alone, not to mention peer groups and affinity groups that are part of the Association of State and Territorial Health Officials and other allied organizations such as the National Association of County and City Health Officials, the Big Cities Health Coalition, CityMatCH (urban maternal and child health programs), the National Environmental Health Association, and others.

These specialty designations have also led to fragmentation within agencies at a time when government is attempting to align more nimbly to meet the needs of the jurisdictions they serve. Few public health professionals have formal training in the skills needed to successfully adapt their work to navigate these changes, especially the strategic skills needed to position their work to meet contemporary public health challenges that require inter- and intra-agency collaboration for success. For example, the pressures and challenges imposed on the public health ecosystem and its workers by the COVID-19 pandemic illustrate the urgency of preparing the public health workforce not just for technical challenges but also for strategic and adaptive challenges posed by novel health threats that require an "all of government" approach to resolve.

Several external forces in recent years, including the movement from Public Health 2.0 to Public Health 3.0 and the six-year-long, three-phased Public Health Workforce Interests and Needs Survey, have either advocated for or implied the need for complementing the workforce's existing discipline-specific expertise with developing a set of strategic skills.

In 2017, the de Beaumont Foundation spearheaded the development of the National Consortium for Public Health Workforce Development comprised of public health leaders from 34 national partner organizations representing a variety of disciplines and settings nationwide. The Consortium was established "to communicate the needs of the front-line public health worker to national partners and funders."[4]

By consensus, the Consortium identified the following nine "indispensable, high-performance skills applicable to the entire public health workforce regardless of specialty or discipline."[5]

- Systems and strategic thinking
- Change management
- Effective communication
- Data-driven decision making
- Community engagement
- Justice, equity, diversity, and inclusion
- Resource management and finance
- Policy engagement
- Cross-sectoral partnerships

These strategic skills are needed by specialty-specific, technical experts in order to realize the multisector, cross-cutting visionary leadership needed today. The Consortium's "call to action" paper asserted this challenge to public health educators: "While maintaining excellence in core scientific disciplines continues to be a priority, developers and deliverers of public health education and training need to act in new and different ways if the governmental public health workforce is to gain competency in the strategic skills needed throughout the entire public health workforce."[5]

Creating these "new and different ways" of building public health workforce competencies in the strategic skills should be a priority for academic programs, professional associations, and public health partners nationwide. This Strategic Skills Series presents a new way to expand the education and training of the public health workforce, equipping its members for multisector collaboration to create policies and programs intended to solve real problems.

To develop this series, we have recruited thought leaders and experts to serve as the authors of each volume. The consistent format applied to each book in the series is intended to facilitate the learner's absorption and retention of key concepts and applications. The practice-based objectives of each book in the series are described below:

- **Systems and strategic thinking:** Grasp patterns and relationships to understand systems contributing to public health problems and identify high-impact interventions.
- **Change management:** Scale programs in response to the changing environments and shape core elements that sustain programs in challenge and crisis.
- **Effective communication:** Convey resonant, compelling public health messages to broad audiences—the public, partners, and policymakers.
- **Data-driven decision making:** Leverage, synthesize, and analyze multiple sources of electronic data and use informatics to identify and act on health priorities, population impacts, evidence-based approaches, and health and cost-related outcomes.
- **Community engagement:** Describe the most effective methods of and the beneficial outcomes from engaging communities in promoting health and well-being. Promote the model of equitable distribution of decision-making power.
- **Justice, equity, diversity, and inclusion:** Understand and respond to the changing demographics of the US population and the public health workforce itself. Seek out, listen to, include, and promote underrepresented populations in reaching effective health solutions.
- **Resource management and finance:** Oversee recruitment, acquisition, and retention of the workforce and manage fiscal resources responsibly.
- **Policy engagement:** Address public health concerns and needs and engage effectively with local, state, and federal policymakers and partners.
- **Cross-sectoral partnerships:** Bring together two or more distinct fields (e.g., health care and transportation) for greater impact so that public health professionals can maintain long-term collaborations that combine a unique set of resources, experience, and knowledge to effectively address multifaceted issues (e.g., the social determinants of health).

As we aim to move public health forward to meet the challenges of contemporary practice, we are excited to edit each of these volumes. It is our fervent hope that each of the books in this series represents a significant brick in the foundation of developing your capacity to address today's urgencies as well as tomorrow's opportunities and challenges.

Michael Fraser, PhD, MS
Brian C. Castrucci, DrPH

REFERENCES

1. Public Health Foundation. Core competencies for public health professionals. 2014. Available at: http://www.phf.org/programs/corecompetencies/Pages/Core_Competencies_Domains.aspx. Accessed January 22, 2021.
2. US Centers for Disease Control and Prevention. 10 essential public health services. 2020. Available at: https://www.cdc.gov/publichealthgateway/publichealthservices/essentialhealthservices.html. Accessed January 22, 2021.

3. Public Health National Center for Innovation. Foundational public health services. 2018. Available at: https://phnci.org/uploads/resource-files/FPHS-Factsheet-November-2018.pdf. Accessed January 22, 2021.
4. de Beaumont Foundation. Building skills for a more strategic public health workforce: a call to action. 2019. Available at: https://debeaumont.org/wp-content/uploads/2019/04/Building-Skills-for-a-More-Strategic-Public-Health-Workforce.pdf. Accessed September 26, 2022.
5. de Beaumont Foundation. Building skills for a more strategic public health workforce: a call to action. July 18, 2017. Available at: https://www.debeaumont.org/news/2017/building-skills-for-a-more-strategic-health-workforce-a-call-to-action. Accessed January 22, 2021.

Preface

We wrote this book together sharing many common bonds—a passion for social justice, public health, and how to pragmatically make the world a healthier place through the power of policy. For us, policy is the key to ensuring that everyone can thrive wherever they live, work, learn, pray, or play.

One of our other shared loves is sports. We have competed, coached, and cheered in many athletic roles. We have played at all levels, from community pick-up games to international competitions. We have studied sports with great fanaticism, so much so that one of us is on a quest to watch a game at every professional US baseball stadium. We routinely root for the underdog, perhaps because we ourselves have been David fighting Goliath – undersized, underfunded, and, often, underestimated. We know what it takes because we have experienced hard-fought wins, just as we have endured heartbreaking losses. In many ways, the ups and downs of being a sports lover are analogous to the ups and downs of public health and policy engagement.

Between the three of us, we bring decades of experience writing laws, rules, and regulations, leading advocacy campaigns, teaching health policy, and translating evidence into action. We have worked for Democrats, Republicans, and Independents. We have engaged in policy at the local, state, federal, and tribal levels. We have knocked on doors, organized communities, stood in the streets in protest, and made our voices heard by testifying.

In this book, we are going to introduce you to the basics and coach you on the skills needed to get involved and make a difference. It has never been more important for public health professionals to employ the knowledge, tactics, and confidence needed to champion policy improvements that can catalyze healthier, more equitable conditions for us all. As with any team, everyone has an important role to play, and we need to work together to create a united, influential, and impactful public health front.

Let's go, public health. It's our time.

Shelley, Keshia, and Katrina

Acknowledgements

The authors would like to thank the many people who helped make this book happen. We are grateful for the support from the Lerner Center for Public Health Advocacy at the Johns Hopkins Bloomberg School of Public Health, specifically, Martha Ruffin as project coordinator, Amber-Ray Davidson for her graphics, Diane Coraggio for her editorial contributions, and Tunmise Olowojoba for her early research. Kyle Kretzer and Joseph Parsons assisted with footnotes and editorial direction. Susan Polan, Kathryn Leifheit, Ilisa Halpern Paul, David Michaels, Alicia Diaz, and Betsy Southerland shared great stories and insights. Lastly, a shout out to Brian Castrucci, Mike Fraser, and APHA Press for championing advocacy as an essential skill.

Introduction

Imagine if public health science, research, and history were the basis for this country's policies. The United States could be one of the healthiest places on earth. That is not the current reality, but it could be.

Facts alone have never been and will never be enough to produce healthier living conditions. While today's political climate is particularly challenging, with an unprecedented presence of misinformation and a growing mistrust in science, the field of political science has long noted that expert advice does not drive the policy process.[1] Facts must be paired with a nuanced understanding of the political environment, which includes individual policymaker perceptions, outside interest groups (both aligning and opposing), and potential windows of opportunities.[2] We can only build a healthier nation when we combine sound public health research with skillful advocacy to navigate the complex political forces shaping our nation's policy.

WHAT IS ADVOCACY?

The American Public Health Association defines an advocate as "a person who argues for a cause - a supporter or a defender" and to advocate as an "act in support of a particular issue or cause."[3] Arguably, being an advocate is a fundamental part of being a public health professional. "Public health is the science of protecting and improving the health of people and their communities," and "protecting the health of entire populations."[4]

Protecting, defending, making an evidence-based case are routine actions, often in the face of opposition and special interests. Advocacy, in its simplest form, reflects the very ethos of public health.

The public call for enhancing policy engagement has been getting louder and louder. Over the last two decades, the National Academies of Science (NAS) has produced numerous reports that document public health's challenges. NAS cites lack of political will as an overarching theme, pointing to the need for the public health field to become better at policymaker engagement.[5,6] The 2003 Institute of Medicine (now National Academy of Medicine) report, *Who Will Keep the Public Healthy? Educating Public Health Professionals for the 21st Century*, acknowledged that for public health to have a significant impact, the field needs to pay attention to both politics and policy.[7] That's a polite way of saying that we need to step up our advocacy skills and tactics.

The public health workforce has been calling for help too. Surveys of the public health workforce reveal that policy engagement is seen as a critically needed skill, one which most public health workers lack proficiency in.[8] For governmental public health managers, supervisors, and executives, policy engagement skills are a top priority.[8] A recent Network for Public Health Law report called for advocacy training at all educational levels (undergraduate, graduate, and professional development) to ensure that public health voices and expertise are embedded in the public discourse and overcome the field's skittishness about policy advocacy.[9]

OVERCOMING THE OBSTACLES

Public health professionals have not always been timid about policy advocacy. In the mid-nineteenth century, public health emerged as a powerful political force that battled social injustices and waves of infectious diseases that threatened the nation's physical health and economic progress. It was the time of anti-slavery and women's rights movements in the United States. Extensive political investments were made in public health, including comprehensive sanitation systems, public water supplies, and strong health departments with vast authority.[10] Public health officials and professionals were highly engaged in the political arena to advance new scientific discoveries and address societal ills. The term *public health* was coined at that time to signal the governmental actions needed to protect the population's health.[11]

Over time, however, public health as a field of practice began to shy away from political dynamics. Starting with the percieved mishandling of 1976 Swine Flu outbreak[12] public health officials have faced political backlash on a variety of health matters. In the past few decades, members of Congress have challenged the Centers for Disease Control and Prevention (CDC) for what has been perceived as overstepping its authority (dare we mention the mask mandates during the COVID-19 pandemic!). Grant programs that engaged in community support or policy assessment were questioned, causing CDC to provide more careful guidance to its grantees on the appropriate use of federal funds.[13] Subsequently, many public health agencies became more cautious about policy engagement. Some public health professionals, from scientists to governmental officials, became apprehensive about partaking in policy development for fear of violating laws or negatively impacting their careers. To this day, some incorrectly perceive advocacy as synonymous with bias or a lack of objectivity.

Too often, public health professionals ask how we can depoliticize public health; however, this is not the question that needs answering. Instead, we need to become proficient at engaging in the political and policymaking process to ensure public health has a seat at the table from the beginning. As we continue to witness converging public health crises, including ever-evolving pandemics, racism, and climate change, it has never been more important for the public health profession to engage in political discourse and policy change. Public health professionals need to take inspiration from the successful 1848 social justice-oriented public health movement and exercise their old advocacy muscles. As a former CDC Washington official noted:

> Public health officials cannot simply ignore the political system because in reality nearly all governmental public health activity is based on authority and funding that is provided through a political decision-making process, usually through enactment of legislation. The ability of federal, state, and local public health officials to regulate, implement programs, spend public money, or receive private funding through user fees or other means is derived through a political process. Furthermore, the aspiration of public health officials to influence policies that *impact* health—such as housing, transportation, and other social and economic determinants—will continue to rely on decision-making by legislators and other elected officials, many of them who do not consider themselves connected to the health system.[14]

Essentially, policymakers need public health professionals in all facets of the policymaking process. Whether you are an academic, a governmental official, or working in the field, you have valuable insights and experience, and there is a role for you. It does not matter if you are the state health commissioner or a bench scientist, your knowledge and expertise can influence the decision-making process. Legislators and other decision-makers (i.e., any person with power and authority to influence or determine actions, policies, and practices at the federal, state, or local level) rarely have the research skills or time needed to review the data and formulate evidence-informed policies. They need public health professionals to translate the science, provide counsel, and propose recommendations and solutions based on high quality research.[15,16] Moreover, they also need public health professionals to be dependable when fights get tough. The more public health professionals are engaged in the policymaking process, the greater influence and impact we can have on the public's health.

CHANGE IS HAPPENING: THIS BOOK IS ONE CATALYZING STEP

While the public health field has limited resources in regard to access to training, continuing education, and even support for policy engagement,[9] changes are on the horizon. The national organization that accredits public health schools and programs, the Council for Education of Public Health (CEPH), maps out the basic competencies that students are expected to acquire. Graduates of public health programs are now expected to have the skills needed to "advocate for political, social, or economic policies and programs that will improve health in diverse populations." This extends beyond a basic ability to make a case for or against a position. By CEPH standards, the next generation of public health leaders must have the comprehensive knowledge and skills needed "to influence policy and/or decision-making, such as through stakeholder mobilization, educating policymakers, etc.... Students must produce a product that would be part of an advocacy campaign or effort (e.g., legislative testimony, fact sheets, advocacy strategy outline, etc.)."[17(p18)]

Many leading public health institutions have invested in this work already. In 2018, the Johns Hopkins Bloomberg School of Public Health revitalized its strategic plan to include advocacy as one of its core goals, including comprehensive training and faculty awards for policy engagement.[18] They also offer a certificate program in public health advocacy. Boston University created the Activist Lab, which provides resources for students to learn the skills necessary to engage in advocacy, activism, and social justice, as well as offering a variety of related practicums, fellowships, and advocacy workshops.[19] Many professional organizations offer advocacy trainings as part of their membership, including the American Public Health Association (APHA) and the Association of Public Health Laboratories. However, much more is needed, especially when it comes to building the capacity of professionals already on the front lines.

This book will introduce you to the who, what, how, when, and where to engage in the policymaking process as a public health professional. The goal is to offer a practical field guide to the unwritten rules, lessons, and insights needed to be successful.

While most insights, strategies, and tactics discussed in this book can easily be applied to international policy engagement, we will focus exclusively on US policies. We will target the skills and strategies needed to engage in the process of translating policies into action by directly engaging, informing, and influencing policymakers in the legislative, regulatory, and budgetary spheres. This book will not cover how to use legal courts to advance policymaking or strategies for influencing business or private sector policies. It is not a substitute for comprehensive advocacy curriculum in public health schools and programs. Rather, it is designed to provide public health professionals with the basic tools for playing an impactful role in shaping policies that improve the health of communities.

When asked at the 2021 AcademyHealth conference how to get politics out of public health, Georges C. Benjamin, MD, MACP, APHA's executive director, answered, "If you do policy, you do politics."[20] This field guide is the first step to help you roll up your sleeves and dive into public health policy with confidence.

Key Takeaways

- Policymakers need help from public health professionals to understand the science behind public health issues and develop solutions based on high-quality research. This cooperative relationship will ensure that health evidence and its impact are a part of how policies are shaped, implemented, funded, and enforced.
- Advocacy skills are being incorporated into competency requirements and are becoming a foundational skill expected of graduates of public health programs.
- The more public health professionals are engaged in the policymaking process, the greater influence and impact we will have on the public's health.

REFERENCES

1. Camargo K Jr, Grant, R. Public health, science, and policy debate: being right is not enough. *Am J Public Health*. 2015;105(2):232–235. Available at: https://doi.org/10.2105/AJPH.2014.302241. Accessed February 2, 2023.
2. Kingdon JW. *Agendas, Alternatives, and Public Policies: Updated Edition With an Epilogue on Health Care*. 2nd ed. London, UK: Pearson; 2011.
3. American Public Health Association. Get the facts on advocacy at APHA. 2022. Available at: https://www.apha.org/policies-and-advocacy/advocacy-for-public-health/coming-to-dc/get-the-facts-on-advocacy-at-apha. Accessed February 2, 2023.
4. CDC Foundation. What is public health? 2023. Available at: https://www.cdcfoundation.org/what-public-health. Accessed February 2, 2023.
5. Committee for the Study of the Future of Public Health, Division of Health Care Services, Institute of Medicine. The future of public health. National Academy Press; 1988. Available at: https://doi.org/10.17226/1091. Accessed July 11, 2022.
6. Committee on Assuring the Health of the Public in the 21st Century, Board on Health Promotion and Disease Prevention, Institute of Medicine of the National Academies. The future of the public's health in the 21st century. National Academies Press; 2003. Available at: https://doi.org/10.17226/10548. Accessed July 11, 2022.
7. Committee on Educating Public Health Professionals for the 21st Century, Board on Health Promotion and Disease Prevention, Institute of Medicine of the National Academies. Who will keep the public healthy? Educating public health professionals for the 21st century. National Academies Press; 2003. Available at: https://doi.org/10.17226/10542. Accessed July 11, 2022.
8. de Beaumont Foundation, Association of State and Territorial Health Officials. Public health workforce interests and needs survey: 2021 dashboard. 2022. Available at: https://www.phwins.org/national. Accessed October 30, 2022.
9. Frey Evaluation LLC. Fighting for public health: findings, opportunities, and next steps from a feasibility study to strengthen public health advocacy. Network for Public Health Law. September 2022. Available at: https://www.networkforphl.org/wp-content/uploads/2022/09/Fight-for-Public-Health-Findings-Opportunities-and-Next-Steps-from-a-Feasibility-Study-to-Strengthen-Public-Health-Advocacy.pdf. Accessed November 18, 2022.
10. Duffy J. *The Sanitarians: A History of American Public Health*. Urbana, IL: University of Illinois Press; 1992.
11. Krieger N, Birn A-E. A vision of social justice as the foundation of public health: commemorating 150 years of the Spirit of 1848. *Am J Public Health*. 1998;88(11):1603–1606. Available at: https://ajph.aphapublications.org/doi/pdf/10.2105/AJPH.88.11.1603. Accessed October 30, 2022.
12. Swine flu of 1976: lessons from the past. *Bull World Health Organ*. 2009;87(6):414–415. Available at: https://www.ncbi.nlm.nih.gov/pmc/articles/PMC2686218. Accessed January 2, 2023.
13. Levinson DR. Letter regarding the CPPW program. Dept of Health and Human Services, Office of the Inspector General. June 29, 2012. Available at: https://www.scribd.com/document/99735795/2012-07-09-HHS-IG. Accessed July 11, 2022.
14. Hunter EL. Politics and public health—engaging the third rail. *J Public Health Manag Pract*. 2016;22(5):436–441. Available at: https://doi.org/10.1097/PHH.0000000000000446. Accessed July 11, 2022.

15. Oliver K, Innvar S, Lorenc T, Woodman J, Thomas J. A systematic review of barriers to and facilitators of the use of evidence by policymakers. *BMC Health Serv Res.* 2014;14. Available at: https://doi.org/10.1186/1472-6963-14-2. Accessed July 11, 2022.
16. Dobbins M, Rosenbaum P, Plews N, Law M, Fysh A. Information transfer: what do decision makers want and need from researchers? *Implement Sci.* 2007;2(20):1–12. Available at: https://doi.org/10.1186/1748-5908-2-20. Accessed July 11, 2022.
17. Council on Education for Public Health. Accreditation criteria: schools of public health and public health programs. Council on Education for Public Health. Amended 2021. Available at: https://ceph.org/documents/297/2021.Criteria.pdf. Accessed October 30, 2022.
18. Johns Hopkins Bloomberg School of Public Health. The power of public health: a strategic plan for the future. Available at: https://publichealth.jhu.edu/sites/default/files/2021-08/jhsph-strategic-plan-abridged.pdf. Accessed January 2, 2023.
19. Activist Lab. Boston University School of Public Health. Available at: https://www.bu.edu/sph/practice/activist-lab. Accessed January 2, 2023.
20. Sanchez E, Hearne S, Avula D, Benjamin G. Closing plenary: reimagining public health. Plenary session at: AcademyHealth Annual Research Meeting; June 14–17, 2021; a virtual event.

1

Policy Matters and So Do You

Everywhere you look, there are policies that affect health. Does your neighborhood have sidewalks that allow you to move safely to key locations, like supermarkets and doctors' offices, without risking death? Does your city or town provide accessible, high-quality pre-K education, which is known to have a substantial impact on a child's future health and well-being?[1] Did your state apply for federal Medicaid expansion resources so that more citizens without insurance have healthcare access? What, if any, are the taxes on tobacco, alcohol, and sugar-sweetened beverages, and how are these funds utilized? Is there a neighborhood nearby that has lower life expectancies, higher disease burdens, or inadequate housing conditions that hinder the community's well-being? All of these reflect policy decisions that shape the health outcomes of our communities and environments.

Policy can take the form of "a law, regulation, procedure, administrative action, incentive, or voluntary practice of governments and other institutions."[2] An enormous range of policies impacting health are routinely made by towns, cities, counties, state and federal agencies, Congress, and even in corporate board rooms.

Many of public health's greatest achievements over the twenty-first century have been driven by major successes in governmental policy (see Table 1-1).[3] For example, tobacco related deaths dropped substantially in part due to imposing taxes and enacting smoking bans in public places. Motor vehicle–related deaths and injuries were reduced as a result of seat belt laws, safety regulations requiring features such as airbags and rearview cameras, and transportation policies requiring smarter highway and traffic design. Lead poisoning prevention laws and regulations, such as the disclosure of the presence of lead-based paint, have resulted in healthier homes and reduced the risk of lead poisoning among many children.[4] Though policy has proven to be a powerful prescription for addressing health problems, great disparities by race, ethnicity, and income remain.

IT DOESN'T HAVE TO SAY HEALTH TO IMPACT HEALTH

Policies developed in sectors outside of the health sector can heavily influence what is known as the *social determinants of health* (SDOH). SDOH refers to the conditions in places where people live, work, learn, play, and pray and the role they have on impacting health, well-being, and quality of life. For example, transportation policies related to pedestrian- and bicycle-friendly community design can encourage or limit physical activity. Education policies have the ability to improve or decrease the nutritional quality of school meals. Housing policies can also have unexpected implications for public health

Table 1-1. The 21st Century's Leading Health Wins Are Associated With Policy Enactment

Health Win	Policies Associated With 21st Century Win
Infectious disease control	Mandatory reporting, TB exam, vaccine mandates for school enrollment
Motor vehicle safety	State speed limits, federal auto requirements (seat belts, air bags, rear view cameras), transportation policies for highways and traffic design, 0.08 BAC limit laws to reduce drunk driving
Safer and healthier foods	FDA and USDA laws, local health department restaurant inspections
Safer workplaces	OSHA standards for lockout/tagout, ROPS, and fall protection
Tobacco control	Taxes, package labeling, age restrictions (T21)
Family planning	Roe v. Wade, ACA expanded coverage to all FDA-approved contraceptive methods

Note: ACA = Affordable Care Act; BAC = blood alcohol concentration; FDA = Food and Drug Administration; OSHA = Occupational Safety and Health Administration; ROPS = rollover protective structures; TB = tuberculosis; T21 = Tobacco 21; USDA = US Department of Agriculture.

as noted in the example in Box 1-1.[5] Since health and well-being are impacted by the SDOH, it is critical that public health professionals pay attention to and influence policies that are formulated and implemented by other sectors.

Policies can also have harmful consequences—unintended or not—if not properly developed or implemented. Governments and other institutions have long sanctioned laws, rules, and practices that are inherently racist, resulting in health disparities.[6] For example, government-sponsored *redlining*, a discriminatory policy that withheld loans and other services from certain racial and ethnic neighborhoods, has had long-term, harmful impacts. In addition to severe financial and social harm, these unjust practices

Box 1-1. Policy Engagement Can Emerge in Unexpected Ways

> At the beginning of the pandemic, Kathryn Leifheit, then a postdoctoral fellow at UCLA Fielding School of Public Health, conducted research that played a pivotal role in influencing the decision to extend eviction moratoriums while the country tried to prevent COVID-related deaths. As the pandemic began to unfold in March 2020, states across the country froze evictions. However, state eviction moratoriums only lasted for 10 weeks on average, which was not sufficient for the millions who could not afford to pay rent during the initial wave of the COVID-19 pandemic. This situation allowed Kathryn and Johns Hopkins researchers to conduct a natural experiment, which found an association between expiring eviction moratoriums and increased COVID-19 incidence and mortality.[5]
>
> Kathryn engaged with key stakeholders and policymakers in many ways, including testifying before city councils and state legislatures, signing legal briefs supporting CDC's federal eviction moratoriums, and translating research for nonprofit housing organizations, who wrote op-eds and lobbied for tenant protections. Kathryn worked on a multidisciplinary team and her collaborator, a legal expert with deep connections to local, state, and national policymakers and advocates, brokered many of these opportunities for policy engagement. This work ended up being in background documents for the federal government's decisions. The research team's powerful findings, timeliness, and the credible translation of scientific implications helped protect millions of people amidst the crisis.

Source: Based on Kathryn M. Leifheit, PhD, MSPH, from a Zoom interview with Tunmise Olowojoba (February 18, 2022).[5] Used with permission of Kathryn M. Leifheit.

have contributed to elevated rates of preterm birth, cancer, tuberculosis, maternal depression, and other mental health issues in historically redlined areas.[6] One of the greatest public health crises of our time is the enormous disparity in health and well-being between races due to a combination of factors, such as, discrimination, institutional and structural racism, oppression, and income inequality. Examples are widespread. We know that Black mothers die during childbirth at three times the rate of white mothers,[7] and their babies are twice as likely to die.[8] The COVID-19 pandemic served as a clear example—people of color, working service jobs, without sick leave, and without proper personal protective equipment died at a disproportionately higher rate than whites and reported greater pandemic-related stressors.[9,10] Of course, we see disparities across many other groups, such as the LGBTQIA+ community, the rural poor, and even between neighborhoods in a single city. If public health is to directly confront inequities caused by oppressive practices and structural racism, we must go beyond addressing individual attitudes and behaviors and engage in the policy process.

POLICY AS THE PRESCRIPTION

We face a broad array of health challenges today that could be improved through policy. The good news is that we have many known, high-impact policy solutions, and we are constantly refining evidence to enhance existing policies or make the case for new ones. For instance, the Centers for Disease Control and Prevention (CDC) established the Health Impact in 5 Years (HI-5) initiative, which identified fourteen public health interventions that are known to be evidence-based, high-impact, and cost-effective.[11] This includes alcohol pricing policies, which are shown to reduce liver cirrhosis, motor vehicle injuries and death, and violence. It also includes earned income tax credits, which are associated with a reduction in infant mortality and preterm births, and improvements in birthweight and maternal mental health.[12]

Unfortunately, strong, evidence-based policies do not always make it to the implementation phase. There may be significant political, social, fiscal, or administrative headwinds to overcome. For example, for years, bars were exempt from smoking bans because of spurious arguments claiming it would hurt business. In other instances, stiff public opposition can lead policymakers to hesitate even if the science is clear, as was the case with mask and vaccine mandates in many parts of the United States during COVID-19. In many situations, despite good data, the uptake of public health policies is unequal to nonexistent. Again, consider tobacco, which remains the leading preventable cause of death, disability, and disease in the United States. The evidence is unequivocal that tobacco restriction policies, such as comprehensive indoor smoking bans and cigarette tax increases, reduce teen smoking, get people to quit, and save lives. Yet numerous US locations have failed to put in place these proven policies. Figure 1-1 shows how variable these laws are from state to state.[13]

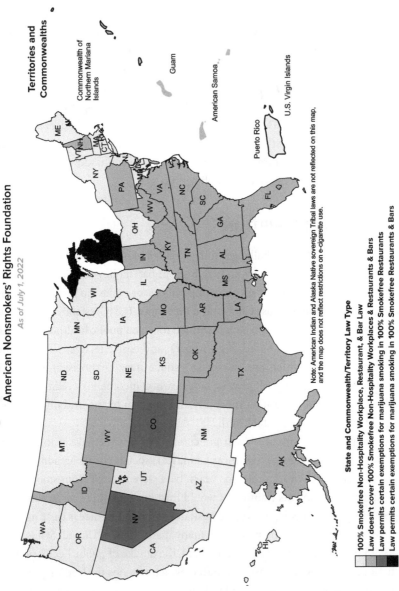

Source: American Nonsmokers' Rights Foundation.[13] Reprinted with permission.

Figure 1-1. Variability of Basic Smoke-Free Laws

In 2022, 38% of the US population lived in places that lack comprehensive smoke-free workplace laws at the state or local level.[14] Who suffers most when high impact policies are absent? Less privileged and historically marginalized and oppressed groups are often the most impacted. For instance, people of color disproportionately work in the hospitality industry, from hotels to casinos, which are routinely exempted from smoke-free laws. And according to CDC, Black children and adults are more likely to be exposed to secondhand smoke than any other racial group.[15]

WHERE (AND WHEN) IS THE BEST PLACE TO ENGAGE IN THE POLICYMAKING PROCESS?

Once public health professionals decide to engage in the policy process, it is critical to determine where and when we can most effectively engage in dialogue with policymakers. The policy process is cyclical, and engagement can occur at every stage of the process.

CDC created a wheel chart showing the five different phases of the policymaking process from conceptualization to implementation (see Figure 1-2).[16] Stakeholder

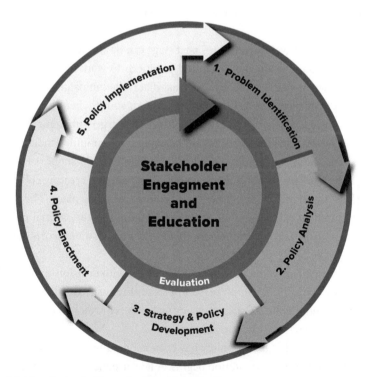

Source: Reprinted from Centers for Disease Control and Prevention.[16]

Figure 1-2. Centers for Disease Control and Prevention Schematic for the Policymaking Process

engagement and education are center stage. They are the heart and soul of effective policymaker engagement for the public health world.

Public health experts have routinely engaged in the first two phases, which are problem identification and policy analysis. This is what we have been trained to do and we do it well.

1. Problem identification: This stage is a core function of public health. Governmental, community-based, and academic public health professionals regularly collect and assess surveillance data. We solicit community concerns and conduct investigations to better understand health risks and the causes of a health problem.
2. Policy analysis: This stage is when potential policy options are considered to determine which are most effective and realistic. This stage is an opportunity to examine how policies may cause or further impact inequities related to intersecting social categories such as race, class, sexuality, and ability.[17] Public health experts, community leaders, academics, businesses, agency officials, and political officeholders routinely conduct this work to determine what policies are possible and viable from their perspective.

    Public health professionals have long been comfortable with providing research and analysis as described above but are less comfortable with the full spectrum of policymaking.
3. Strategy and policy development: This next stage can be considered the action phase, which is when you pull together allies and coalitions to work together on a targeted policy. This is when we ask questions, such as what is the campaign strategy to inform and engage policymakers to get the policy enacted; and if/when the policy gets put into place, how do public health officials ensure that it gets implemented properly? This phase entails working with key stakeholders—community members, subject matter experts, campaign leaders—to develop a plan to build support for the policy recommendation. This includes crafting policy language and creating collateral materials, such as health impact assessments and communications plans. The full array of policy development skills is outlined in more detail in the 10 essential public health services (see Figure 1-3),[18] a framework that centers equity and incorporates current and future public health practice.
4. Policy enactment: This is the time to actively engage with decision-makers who have the authority to put a policy in place. Examples of this are getting legislatures to pass a law, working with public officials to decide on budgets or rules, or collaborating with board members to write corporate policies.
5. Policy implementation: Once a policy has been adopted by the official deciders, the challenging phase of implementation begins. A law or policy can be a broad mandate or charge, and the specific details for putting the policy into action are critical. What are the details of the budget that support the policy? How will the law be enforced?

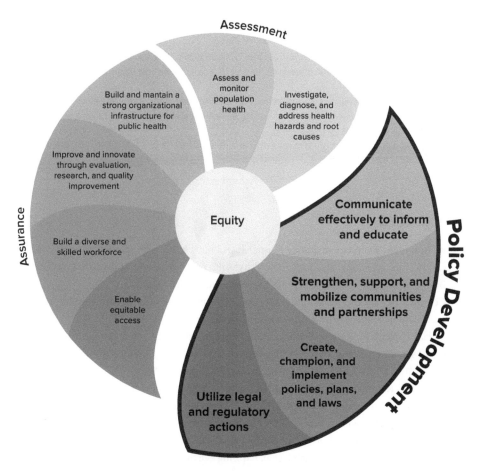

Source: Reprinted from Public Health National Center for Innovations.[18]

Figure 1-3. The Policy Development Component of the 10 Essential Public Health Services

What specific chemicals or diseases are covered under a new environmental or health law? This phase is an enormous opportunity for public health professionals to have an impact.

As noted in the CDC wheel's second ring, evaluation is core to every step. Evaluating the study of the impacts, outcomes, and costs of a policy lets us know how well it is working in practice.

A strong public health policy must be deeply rooted in evidence, but evidence is just the beginning. Good science is necessary but not sufficient for success. Advancing a policy from theory into practice requires a deep understanding of and appreciation for the intricacies of the political process. The more in tune we are with policymaking systems, the more likely we are to succeed at improving health and well-being for all.

> **Key Takeaways**
> - Public health professionals are needed in all facets of the decision-making process.
> - Many of public health's greatest achievements over the 21st century have been driven by major successes in governmental policy.
> - Look beyond public health laws and regulations. Pay attention to and influence policies that are formulated and implemented by other sectors, such as housing, transportation, and education, that can have significant health impacts.
> - Advancing a policy from theory into practice requires a deep understanding of and appreciation for the intricacies of the political process.

REFERENCES

1. de Beaumont Foundation, Kaiser Permanente. Policy brief: high-quality, accessible pre-K. CityHealth. Available at: https://www.cityhealth.org/wp-content/uploads/2021/10/Policy-Brief-High-Quality-Access-Pre-K.pdf. Accessed November 13, 2022.
2. Centers for Disease Control and Prevention. CDC policy process. Available at: https://www.cdc.gov/policy/analysis/process. Accessed November 13, 2022.
3. Pollack Porter KM, Rutkow L, McGinty EE. The importance of policy change for addressing public health problems. *Public Health Rep*. 2018;133(Suppl 1):9S–14S. Available at: https://doi.org/10.1177/0033354918788880. Accessed November 13, 2022.
4. Dignam T, Kaufmann RB, LeStrourgeon L, Brown MJ. Control of lead sources in the United States, 1970–2017: public health progress and current challenges to eliminating lead exposure. *J Public Health Manag Pract*. 2019;25:S13–S22. Available at: https://doi.org/10.1097/PHH.0000000000000889. Accessed November 13, 2022.
5. Leifheit KM, Linton SL, Raifman J, et al. Expiring eviction moratoriums and COVID-19 incidence and mortality. *Am J Epidemiol*. 2021;190(12):2503–2510. Available at: https://doi.org/10.1093/aje/kwab196. Accessed November 13, 2022.
6. Bailey ZD, Feldman JM, Bassett MT. How structural racism works—racist policies as a root cause of US racial health inequities. *N Engl J Med*. 2021;384(8):768–773. Available at: https://www.nejm.org/doi/full/10.1056/NEJMms2025396. Accessed November 13, 2022.
7. Centers for Disease Control and Prevention. Working together to reduce black maternal mortality. April 6, 2022. Available at: https://www.cdc.gov/healthequity/features/maternal-mortality/index.html. Accessed February 7, 2023.
8. Centers for Disease Control and Prevention. Infant mortality. June 22, 2022. Available at: https://www.cdc.gov/reproductivehealth/maternalinfanthealth/infantmortality.htm#about. Accessed February 9, 2023.
9. Gould E, Wilson V. Black workers face two of the most lethal preexisting conditions for coronavirus—racism and economic inequality. Economic Policy Institute. June 1, 2020. Available at: https://www.epi.org/publication/black-workers-covid. Accessed February 8, 2023.

10. Haro-Ramos AY, Brown TT, Deardorff J, Aguilera A, Pollack Porter KM, Rodriguez HP. Frontline work and racial disparities in social and economic pandemic stressors during the first COVID-19 surge. *Health Serv Res*. January 31, 2023. Available at: https://doi.org/10.1111/1475-6773.14136. Accessed November 13, 2022.
11. Skillen E, Hearne S. Building off of evidence-based policies: the CDC's Health Impact in 5 Years (HI-5) initiative and CityHealth, an initiative of the de Beaumont Foundation and Kaiser Permanente. In: Michener JL, Castrucci BC, Bradley DW, et al., eds. *The Practical Playbook II: Building Multisector Partnerships that Work*. Oxford, UK: Oxford University Press; 2019:407–424.
12. Centers for Disease Control and Prevention. The HI-5 interventions. 2021. Available at: https://www.cdc.gov/policy/opaph/hi5/interventions/index.html. Accessed November 13, 2022.
13. American Nonsmokers' Rights Foundation. Smokefree lists and maps quarterly update—October 2021. Available at: https://no-smoke.org/smokefree-lists-and-maps-quarterly-update-october-2021/#. Accessed November 13, 2022.
14. American Nonsmokers' Rights Foundation. Smokefree threats. 2022. Available at: https://no-smoke.org/smokefree-threats. Accessed March 8, 2022.
15. Homa DM, Neff LJ, King BA, et al. Vital signs: disparities in nonsmokers' exposure to secondhand smoke—United States, 1999–2012. *MMWR Morb Mortal Wkly Rep*. 2015;64(4):103–108. Available at: https://www.cdc.gov/mmwr/preview/mmwrhtml/mm6404a7.htm?s_cid=mm6404a7_w. Accessed July 11, 2022.
16. Centers for Disease Control and Prevention. The CDC policy process. 2019. Available at: https://www.cdc.gov/policy/polaris/policyprocess/index.html. Accessed November 13, 2022.
17. Hankivsky O, Grace D, Hunting G, et al. An intersectionality-based policy analysis framework: critical reflections on a methodology for advancing equity. *Int J Equity Health*. 2014;13:119. Available at: https://equityhealthj.biomedcentral.com/articles/10.1186/s12939-014-0119-x#citeas. Accessed November 13, 2022.
18. Public Health National Center for Innovations. The 10 essential public health services. 2020. Available at: https://phnci.org/uploads/resource-files/EPHS-English.pdf. Accessed February 2, 2023.

2

A Look Into Where Policy Is Made

Policy refers to a standard set of principles that guide a course of action.[1] Policy can take many forms, including private or institutional policies created by organizations for institutional use (e.g., personnel related policies) and public policies established by the government. Policies may be legally binding—as in the case of legislation or statutory law—regulations promulgated by federal, state, or local administrative agencies, or even case law, which is created through judicial opinions.[2] Policies may also be enacted via executive order, as we often see from US presidents, especially when there is gridlock in Congress.

This chapter provides a snapshot of the governmental policy landscape and identifies the opportunities and interventions to inform these decisions. As we focus on these policies, we are reminded of one scholar who simplified public policy to be "anything a government chooses to do or not to do."[3(p2)]

THE BASICS OF GOVERNMENT POLICYMAKING PROCESS

Fundamentally, policies are derived from three branches of government: legislative, executive, and judicial. This structure, described below, typically exists at the local, state, and federal levels, each with different names, roles, and authorities. Tribal governments are unique in that they determine their own government structures, policies, and laws. Because of this self-governance, policy engagement with tribes must involve strong partnerships with tribal nations.[4]

- Legislative: The part of the government that makes laws, such as a city council, state assembly, or Congress. Legislatures also pass budgets determining how much money is given to specific branches of government. A law may be passed, but if funding is inadequate, a policy will likely fail.
- Executive: The executive branch has the responsibility of implementing the laws by developing rules and regulations, staffing to get the job done, and enforcement. In cities, the executive is typically the mayor, counties have a county executive or administrator, and states have governors. The United States has a president at the federal level. Each executive oversees the administrative entities responsible for running that jurisdictional government, such as a transportation department, a health agency, and law enforcement authorities.

- Judicial: This branch interprets the law. While judicial policymaking can be seen as controversial, the interpretation of laws and statutes routinely helps define and set guidelines for agency or legislative action. Courts are present in local municipalities, all the way up to the federal circuit level, with the Supreme Court being the final arbitrator on federal law (referring to the Constitution and laws passed by Congress).

These three branches of government are intended to provide checks and balances on each other. Policies can emerge from all of them. All levels of government have some powers that are concurrent, such as the authority to impose taxes or build roads, but not everything is equal. If federal, state, or local laws come into conflict, the higher level of government wins—its authority supersedes and takes precedence over the lower level of government. This has become known as *preemption*, which has many public health implications, both good and bad (see Box 2-1).[5-7]

The Affordable Care Act (ACA) illustrates the interactive policymaking roles of each governmental branch.

- Congressional: Congress was responsible for writing and passing the legislation for the ACA. To inform this process, congressional committees held over 70 hearings, roundtables, and summits to understand healthcare funding issues from the different perspectives of patients, doctors, insurers, and public health professionals. Public health associations, experts, and individuals engaged in various ways by advising policymakers, writing model language, researching outcomes based on different policy options, providing testimony, and participating in town halls and marching in demonstrations.[8-10]
- Executive: President Obama, who championed healthcare reform, signed the bill into law and directed his executive branch agencies to craft the rules and regulations governing that act's implementation. Aided by the Internal Revenue Service and the Employee Benefits Security Administration, the Centers for Medicaid and Medicare Services in the US Department of Health and Human Services (HHS) created 265 regulatory actions to cover components ranging from pre-existing conditions to coverage for contraceptive services.[11,12]

Box 2-1. Masking Health Preemption Preventing Local Policy

On July 8, 2020, at the height of the COVID-19 pandemic, then Atlanta Mayor Keisha Lance Bottoms issued an executive order requiring all persons within the city of Atlanta to wear a mask or cloth face covering over their nose and mouth in response to the rising COVID-19 cases.[5] The order also prohibited gatherings of more than 10 persons on municipal property. On July 16, 2020, Georgia Governor Brian Kemp sued the Atlanta City Council and Mayor Bottoms, arguing that the city's policy violated his executive order, which strongly encouraged mask wearing but did not require it.[6,7] Though the lawsuit was later dropped, in August 2021 Governor Kemp issued an executive order prohibiting local governments in Georgia from imposing mask, vaccine, or building-capacity mandates aimed at discouraging the spread of COVID-19. The Governor's actions curtailed and effectively preempted Georgia municipalities' ability to slow the spread of the virus.

- Judicial: The courts, including the Supreme Court, reviewed numerous legal cases following the passage of the ACA, challenging aspects of the law like the constitutionality of the individual mandate. Since 2010, the ACA has been challenged nearly 2,000 times in state and federal courts. The Supreme Court ruled in favor of the ACA's individual mandate but struck down its expansion of Medicaid in June of 2012.[13(pp168-169),14]

LEGISLATING HEALTH AND HOW YOU CAN ENGAGE IN THIS POLICYMAKING WORLD

From Congress to city councils, elected officials have many tools and techniques for crafting policy. That means you also have many opportunities to engage in shaping policies from testifying at hearings, meeting directly with officials, and more. Legislators are empowered to pass laws, raise and allocate government's financial resources, and provide oversight of the executive branch agencies implementing the laws. Each of these authorities are powerful policy levers that can influence health and well-being.

The Law-Making Process

Generally speaking, the law-making process begins when a bill is first drafted to meet some articulated goal. The bill is then introduced by a sponsor (often with co-sponsors) and referred to a committee. Typically, a subcommittee will review the bill and hold hearings, after which the committee marks it up to the point where amendments may make the bill look very different from where it started. The subcommittee can send the bill to the full committee, which also has the opportunity to debate, amend, and decide to release a revised version of the bill to the entire legislative body to consider. The cycle continues. If a bill makes it out of committee, then legislative leaders determine if it will get a full vote, which may include the debate and introduction of additional amendments. You can imagine how a policy idea in the form of a legislative bill can easily die a thousand different ways.

Once the bill passes one chamber (namely the House or the Senate), it is referred to the other chamber where it undergoes a similar process. This chamber may approve the bill as is, reject it, ignore it, or change it. Sometimes a conference committee may be formed to resolve differences between each chamber's version of a bill. If an agreement is not reached, the bill dies (which is typical in a highly partisan climate). If an agreement is reached and the executive signs the bill, the bill becomes law. In this case, the committee members prepare a conference report with recommendations for the final bill. Both chambers approve the conference report, and then, at the federal level, the bill goes to the president for signature. There is a similar flow of steps for the legislative process at the state level and the local level, which involves a city or county council. Regardless of the level at which you are working, it is important to have a solid understanding of the various steps in the law-making process so that you know where opportunities for engagement exist.

The law-making process related to health is a little more complicated because bills affecting the various drivers of health or social determinants of health are present across many committees. In a confusing, mix-and-match process, a federal bill with health implications could be assigned to any of the 23 different House committees or 17 Senate committees. Committees with jarringly different agendas and focus areas could be reviewing and debating identical bills. This means that similar or identical bills are assigned to committees that may differ in their focus area. For example, during the 117th Congress (2021–2022), the Food and Nutrition Education in Schools Act of 2021 was introduced in the House and referred to the House Committee on Education and Labor, while an identical bill introduced in the Senate was referred to the Committee on Agriculture, Nutrition, and Forestry. As you can imagine, the focus and motivations of the committee members are different in these two committees, which impacts how the bills are discussed and debated, as well as the type of evidence that may resonate with committee members.

The Spending Process

Money is a powerful lever. How funds are budgeted and used are policy decisions that can have an enormous impact on health. Did the town council budget prioritize stadiums and street repairs over creating a well-staffed health department, greenways, safe playgrounds, sidewalks, and healthy spaces for children and adults to play and exercise? Were resources given to implement a public health law? Were government dollars used to subsidize or incentivize good health? The bottom line is that the political arena is where critical decisions on public health budgets are made, which is one more reason to engage in the process.

Not only do these budget decisions determine what public health work agencies can do, but the funding can also be used to incentivize policies (see Box 2-2).[15] For instance,

Box 2-2. Lack of Funding Is a Policy Decision

> When CDC's National Center for Injury Prevention and Control began to address gun violence as a public health issue, the National Rifle Association engaged with policymakers to stop these efforts.[15] Starting in 1996, Congress included a provision in CDC's funding authorization that inhibited gun control promotion or advocacy and shifted the agency's violence prevention budget to study traumatic brain injuries. Known as the Dickey Amendment, this provision essentially intimidated CDC, preventing them from funding research related to firearms in virtually any manner. Even when President Obama directed CDC to conduct gun violence research, no shift occurred. For all intents and purposes, Congress had established a two-decades-long policy that had a chilling effect on CDC's engagement in gun violence prevention. In 2019, after a significant push by advocates and a scourge of high-profile school shootings, Congress reversed course, specifically funding both CDC and NIH to sponsor gun violence prevention research.

Note: CDC = Centers for Disease Control and Prevention; NIH = National Institutes of Health.

only states have authority to regulate alcohol, but Congress spurred states to raise the drinking age to 21 by withholding 10% of federal highway funds to those without the law.[16]

In broad strokes, the federal government moves money through two major phases. The first phase is the budget process, which involves both the executive and legislative branches. Think of this as determining the basic allocations for household spending for things like food, utilities, education, health needs, and clothing. The second phase is the congressional appropriations process, which is the equivalent of writing checks within each budget category, similar to using the housing budget to pay the mortgage, insurance, roofing repairs, and so forth.

For the federal government, creating a budget for a single fiscal year can take multiple years (see Figure 2-1 for a sense of the timeline).[17] Each year, all federal agencies go through an extensive planning process to determine proposed budgets. For example, CDC directors map out needs and responsibilities and submit budgets to the agency head who then submits recommendations to HHS, which then submits everything for review to the president's Office of Management and Budget (OMB), throughout the process. In February of each year, the president submits a recommended budget to Congress for the next fiscal year.

At every stage of budget discussions, public health professionals can provide valuable input and perspective. Agency officials routinely look for input and recommendations from public health professionals by using advisory boards, nongovernmental organization reports, and National Academies panels.[17] Agencies incorporate Congressional guidance and requests in addition to their own technical expertise and programmatic knowledge.

The final decision on the budget rests with Congress. As the old adage goes, "The President proposes, the Congress disposes."[17] This legislative process goes through multiple phases. The first phase is establishing the budget resolution, which both the Senate and House must agree on with majority votes. This sets the binding parameters for the second phase in which both legislative bodies hammer out spending details through twelve separate appropriations committees. For health, the Subcommittee on Labor, HHS, Education, and Related Agencies creates a spending bill that covers all the public health agencies, including the National Institutes of Health (NIH) and CDC. Public

Agency Planning												OMB Review				Budget Release	Congressional Budget and Appropriations								
Oct	Nov	Dec	Jan	Feb	Mar	Apr	May	Jun	Jul	Aug	Sep	Oct	Nov	Dec	Jan	Feb	Mar	Apr	May	Jun	Jul	Aug	Sep

Source: American Association for the Advancement of Science.[17] Reprinted with permission.
Note: OMB = Office of Management and Budget.

Figure 2-1. Federal Budget Steps and Timing

Box 2-3. The Budget Whisperer

> "Developing relationships with elected officials and their staff can bear significant fruit: creating a connection with policymakers means often they will seek your opinion and heed your recommendations. Over the course of my more than 30 years of being involved in federal public health advocacy – both as a Senate staffer and as a lobbyist – I have seen first-hand the positive outcome that public health professionals can have on federal funding for public health."

Source: Email from Ilisa Halpern Paul, former lobbyist for American Public Health Association, American Cancer Society, and other leading health organizations, on September 25, 2022. Reprinted with permission.

health professionals can engage with these House and Senate subcommittee members and staff to advocate for critical resources (see Box 2-3).

The Oversight Role of the Legislative Branch

Legislative bodies serve three core functions: representation, legislating (lawmaking), and oversight. Oversight is a continuous and ongoing process, which can take many forms, to ensure that the executive branch and its agencies are accountable. At a high level, legislative oversight involves monitoring, reviewing, inspecting, and supervising executive actions, programs, policies, budgets, and policy implementation. Legislative oversight is an essential check and balance and a core function in the promotion of good governance.

Legislatures conduct their oversight in several ways. You are likely familiar with congressional hearings, or maybe you have testified at a local council. Hearings, whether they are focused on policy, confirmations, the budget, or are investigative in nature, provide a forum for public engagement and allow members of the legislature to improve the efficiency and effectiveness of governmental operations. Hearings also enable fair evaluation of program performance, create space to review and set priorities, and afford members of government an opportunity to acquire information useful for future policymaking.

Hearings are perhaps the most well-known venue for legislative oversight, and there was no more effective purveyor of the oversight process than Representative John Dingell. Congressman Dingell has the distinction of being the longest serving member of Congress in American history, representing the state of Michigan in the US House of Representatives for 59 years. As the Chairman of the House Committee on Energy and Commerce, he was known for his approach to oversight. Notoriously, Dingell would subpoena numerous government officials, insist that they testify under oath before his committee, interrogate them for hours, and subject them to perjury charges if they failed to comply. His dogged approach uncovered many instances of corruption and waste, and helped to cement his legacy.

Hearings are a wonderful entry point to engage with decision-makers and influence policy, but they are not the only form of oversight. Another prominent oversight tactic lies in the extraordinary power of a well-timed and well-written letter. Letters can be an extremely effective lever for accountability. Many legislators share their letters publicly, enabling residents, advocates, and community members to understand the issues and proposed solutions, arming the general public with the information they need to effectively advocate on a specific topic.

On August 24, 2021 the majority of the Council of the District of Columbia wrote a public letter to Mayor Muriel Bowser asking her to issue an updated order to require all public school employees, child care facility employees, and DC government employees who had regular contact with minors to be vaccinated against COVID-19.[18] Just three weeks later on September 20, 2021, the Mayor signed a Mayor's Order requiring that all adults regularly in schools and child care centers in the District must be vaccinated against COVID-19 by November 1, 2021. Through one letter, the Council played a crucial role in creating a citywide policy.

Oversight is an important avenue for the engagement of decision-makers and the development of policy. Public health practitioners are uniquely positioned to identify issues, arm leaders with compelling data and evidence, and craft questions that will help hold the government accountable and influence the outcomes of policy debates.

ADMINISTERING HEALTH POLICIES: HOW AGENCIES PROTECT AND PROMOTE THE PUBLIC'S HEALTH

Businesses have chief executive officers (CEOs) who are charged with managing operations. In government, the executive branch runs the basic everyday functions with the CEOs being elected officials. The United States has a president, states have governors, counties (or, in Louisiana, parishes) have county executives, and towns and cities have mayors. These executives are responsible for implementing and enforcing the laws created by the legislature. Executives appoint individuals to lead the various agencies, which sometimes requires approval by the legislature. While the agencies are typically staffed by nonpartisan bureaucrats who are insulated from politics through civil servant protections, the agency heads are political appointees. As noted in the example in Box 2-4, political transition periods can be a critical time to engage in the policy process. Regardless of position, government employees can have considerable impact on what policies are priorities and how they are shaped and implemented.

Federal Health Agencies

The federal government plays a significant role in overseeing and supporting health programs throughout the country. HHS has eleven agencies, including CDC, FDA,

> **Box 2-4. People Matter**
>
> "In 2020, Inseparable, an advocacy nonprofit newly founded to fundamentally improve mental health care policy, skillfully organized the mental health advocacy field to identify candidates for key department positions after President Biden's election. The goal was to advance mental health policy reform by placing mental health allies into leadership positions where they can change federal policies and direct administrative actions – without requiring congressional approval. A working group of experts in the field met regularly to assemble a list of potential nominees for each position. The result was a binder with each candidate's bio, resume, headshot and relevant social media links, which was shared with the Biden transition team and White House Presidential Personnel Office. Social media and letters of support were used to uplift and advocate for the nominations. These efforts helped yield eight successful high-level HHS and Department of Labor nominations that can champion mental health from inside the government, and shows how political transition periods are a critical time to engage in the policy process."
>
> *Source:* Email from Alicia Diaz, co-founder of Inseparable, on October 4, 2022. Reprinted with permission.

and NIH (see Figure 2-2).[19] They also cover Medicare and Medicaid services. HHS spends more money than any federal agency—more than the Department of Defense or the Social Security Administration.[20] HHS spans a wide array of policy activities, from regulating tobacco, food, and pharmaceuticals to funding personal health services and biomedical research.

Each agency within HHS plays a different role, yet all carry out policies that can be informed and influenced by public health professionals. (See Appendix 2A for a description of each of these agencies.) Some HHS agencies do not play a regulatory role, such as NIH. Nonetheless, these nonregulatory agencies can have a substantial impact on health policy. NIH creates de facto policy about disease priorities by determining what issues to study and where to allocate funds. Aside from working within these agencies, one way for public health professionals to influence nonregulatory policies is to participate in agency advisory committees. Nonregulatory activities and policies are easy to track via the Federal Register, which serves as a daily record for federal agency updates and happenings.[21] Maintained by the National Archives, you visit www.federalregistrar.gov to track what's happening policywise at all federal agencies, search for specific topics and issues, subscribe to get regular updates on activities, or make it part of your daily reading. It's an excellent way to be directly in the know.

Agencies and Their Rulemaking Process: A Key Engagement Opportunity

Rulemaking is one of the most basic tools agencies use to carry out public policy. *Rules* are government statements that carry out or explain a law, a policy, or procedure for implementing a policy. HHS rules can cover a broad range of issues, such as food

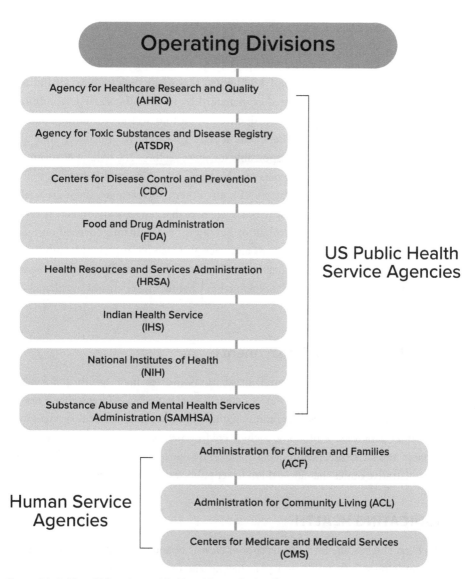

Source: Adapted from US Department of Health and Human Services.[19]
Figure 2-2. US Department of Health and Human Services Organizational Chart

safety standards, health privacy standards, or operating standards for hospitals and day care facilities.[22] Federal law requires that agencies conduct a public comment period as part of the rulemaking process, during which an agency will solicit facts, perspectives, and advice from stakeholders and experts. Public health professionals can have an enormous impact in shaping policies by participating in the public comment period or, even better, proactively engaging with agency staff to help prioritize and shape implementation of laws (see Chapter 6 for more details).

Public health has an important role to play in the rulemaking process outside of HHS and other health agencies. Chapter 1 highlighted that many policies have an indirect impact on health but are not created or managed by health officials. The conditions needed for health and well-being are influenced by various sectors, including housing, transportation, education, and others. The federal government, and many state and local jurisdictions, have agencies responsible for these sectors. The federal government includes the Departments of Transportation, Housing, Education, and Energy, as well as the Environmental Protection Agency and many others. Increasingly, there are health officials that provide health expertise to other agencies that can have an impact on health outcomes. For example, the Department of Energy is predominantly focused on management of the nation's nuclear weapons and energy, which has profound health implications that range from climate impact to worker safety. Public health perspectives and tools, such as "health in all policies" (explained in Chapter 5), are critical in rulemaking and policy processes such as this.

State and Local Health Departments

The structures for how governmental jurisdictions oversee their health and health-related policies vary widely from state to state. Some states have a centralized health department that runs all local operations. Others have separate medical services and public health operations, while some include environmental responsibilities. Regardless of the name and structure, health departments have a broad range of roles, authorities, and administrative duties that allow them to set public health policy (see Figure 2-3).[23]

ADJUDICATING HEALTH

Charles Evan Hughes, the former governor of New York and eventual chief justice of the US Supreme Court, is famously quoted as having said that the Constitution "is what the judges say it is."[24] The statement is a bold assertion as it implies the Constitution is meaningless unless the judges tell us its meaning. It further illuminates a longstanding tension between what the judiciary is designed to do and how it actually functions.

In the United States, law is based first and foremost on the Constitution. Article III of the Constitution establishes the judicial branch. Generally speaking, our courts are empowered to interpret the laws and apply them impartially and without regard for politics. In the Federalist Papers No. 78, Alexander Hamilton wrote:

> The legislature not only commands the purse, but prescribes the rules by which the duties and rights of every citizen are to be regulated. The judiciary, on the contrary, has no

Preparedness & Response
- Disaster Response Management & Coordination
- Hazmat Response
- Poison Control
- Pandemic Response Activities: Contact Tracing, Data Monitoring and Reporting, Genomic Sequencing, Supply Chain Management, Immunization Strategy Development and Implementation, Communication and Education, etc.

Epidemiology & Surveillance
- Managing Data Systems and Tracking Trends for Immunization, Vital Records (birth & death data), and Infectious Disease.
- Cancer, Immunization, Vital Statistics, Chronic Disease, and Other Population Health Registry Maintenance
- Fielding and Analyzing Data for National Surveys (ex. BRFSS, PRAMS)

Disease Prevention & Health Promotion
- Immunization
- Clinical Care Delivery
  - Mental Health Services
  - Substance Use Disorder Treatment
  - Primary Care
  - Oral Health Care
- Managing Collaborative Partnerships to Reduce State Chronic Disease Burden
- Facilitate the Development of Strategies to Address the HIV and Opioid Epidemics

Regulatory Oversight
- Hospitals
- Nursing Homes
- Long Term Care Facilities
- Food Service Establishments
- Water Systems
- Laboratories
- Trauma System Designations
- Body Piercing/Tattoo Parlors
- Septic Tank Systems
- Childcare Facilities

Source: Person et al.[23] Reprinted with permission of ASTHO.
Note: BRFSS = Behavioral Risk Factor Surveillance System; PRAMS = Pregnancy Risk Monitoring System.

Figure 2-3. Range of State Health Agency Activities

influence over either the sword or the purse; no direction either of the strength or of the wealth of the society; and can take no active resolution whatever. It may truly be said to have neither FORCE nor WILL, but merely judgment; and must ultimately depend upon the aid of the executive arm even for the efficacy of its judgments.[25]

It is the emphasis on judgment, rather than will or force, that stands out and begs the question, when does interpretation traverse into dangerous territory, where judges and justices supplant the law of the land in favor of their personal convictions? It is a difficult question, and one made more complicated in our increasingly polarized and politically divided world. While there is little for practitioners to do in the way of engaging the courts, it is nevertheless important to have a general understanding of the role of American courts in shaping and influencing policy. At the federal level, the most important power of the courts is that of *judicial review*, which refers to the authority to interpret the Constitution and determine the constitutional validity of legislative acts. When judges rule that governmental actions or laws violate the spirit and intent of the Constitution, they profoundly shape public policy.

The recent Supreme Court decision in *Dobbs v. Jackson Women's Health Organization* is one example of the role of the courts and their impact on policy. The Dobbs decision overturned both *Roe v. Wade* and *Planned Parenthood v. Casey*, with the highest court holding that the Constitution does not confer a right to abortion. The effects of this decision will be far-reaching and have significant implications for public health.

In 2018, the city of Austin, Texas became the first southern city to pass comprehensive earned sick leave. In time, they were succeeded by Dallas and San Antonio in the adoption of robust earned sick leave policies. However, all three laws were eventually challenged by business groups alleging that the laws violated the State of Texas' minimum wage law, which prohibited localities from enacting a minimum wage higher than the state's. The Texas Court of Appeals ruled that the laws were preempted by the state and, since the Texas Supreme Court declined to hear the case, the ruling of the appellate court stands. In their interpretation of state law, the court unquestionably shaped the policy landscape, leaving residents across Texas without a legal right to paid time off, despite the will of elected leaders and their residents.[26,27]

The merits of what constitute judicial overreach will not be debated in this chapter, but questions about partisan divides raise important ethical questions that we should all be mindful of as we work to engage in the broader policymaking process. Once again, remember that it is critical to engage in the politics of policymaking while remaining nonpartisan, finding facts, champions, and allies from all possible interests. How to do this effectively and with credibility will be the focus of the following chapters.

> **Key Takeaways**
> - Public health professionals are uniquely positioned to identify issues, arm leaders with compelling data and evidence, and craft questions that will help hold policymakers accountable and influence the outcomes of policy debates.
> - Influence can happen at all levels of government, from local to national and from legislatures to administrative agencies.
> - Legislators are empowered to pass laws, raise and allocate the government's financial resources, and provide oversight of the executive branch agencies implementing the laws. This provides public health professionals with many opportunities to engage in shaping policies.
> - Agency decision-making can be a place where public health professionals have the greatest impact. From local to federal, different agencies need input for shaping, overseeing, supporting, and implementing health programs.

REFERENCES

1. Kingdon JW. *Agendas, Alternatives, and Public Policies: Updated Edition With an Epilogue on Health Care*. 2nd ed. London, UK: Pearson; 2011.
2. Pollack Porter KM, Rutkow L, McGinty EE. The importance of policy change for addressing public health problems. *Public Health Rep*. 2018;133(1_suppl):9S–14S. Available at: https://doi.org/10.1177/0033354918788880. Accessed November 29, 2022.
3. Dye TR. *Understanding Public Policy*. Englewood Cliffs, NJ: Prentice Hall; 1972.
4. National Congress of American Indians. Tribal governance. 2023. Available at: https://www.ncai.org/policy-issues/tribal-governance. Accessed February 2, 2023.
5. Mayor's Office of Communications. Mayor Keisha Lance Bottoms issues executive order requiring mask use in all public places while indoors. July 28, 2021. Available at: https://www.atlantaga.gov/Home/Components/News/News/13797/672. Accessed November 29, 2022.
6. State of Georgia. Executive order: empowering a healthy Georgia. July 15, 2020. Available at: https://www.courthousenews.com/wp-content/uploads/2020/07/kemp-july-15-exec-order.pdf. Accessed November 29, 2022.
7. Kemp BP. Complaint for declaratory and injunctive relief: civil action file no.:2020CV__. The Superior Court of Fulton County, State of Georgia. July 16, 2020. Available at: https://www.courthousenews.com/wp-content/uploads/2020/07/kemp-v-bottoms-complaint.pdf. Accessed November 29, 2022.
8. America's Affordable Health Choices Act, HR 3200, 111th Cong (2009). Available at: https://www.congress.gov/111/crpt/hrpt299/CRPT-111hrpt299-pt3.pdf. Accessed November 29, 2022.
9. Health care reform from conception to final passage: timeline of the Finance Committee's work to reform America's health care system. Available at: https://www.finance.senate.gov/imo/media/doc/Health%20Care%20Reform%20Timeline.pdf. Accessed November 29, 2022.
10. Senate Democrats: passage of the Affordable Care Act was open and transparent, with hundreds of hours of public hearings and dozens of committee meetings – after passage of law, health care costs and insurance numbers are proof that ACA works. Chris Murphy. December 9, 2014.

Available at: https://www.murphy.senate.gov/newsroom/press-releases/senate-democrats-passage-of-affordable-care-act-was-open-and-transparent-with-hundreds-of-hours-of-public-hearings-and-dozens-of-committee-meetings_after-passage-of-law-health-care-costs-and-insurance-numbers-are-proof-that-aca-works. Accessed November 29, 2022.
11. Haeder SF, Yackee SW. Regulation, delegation, and the Affordable Care Act. *Regulatory Review*. August 4, 2020. Available at: https://www.theregreview.org/2020/08/04/haeder-yackee-regulation-delegation-affordable-care-act. Accessed November 29, 2022.
12. Kessler G. How many pages of regulations for "Obamacare"? *Washington Post*. May 15, 2013. Available at: https://www.washingtonpost.com/blogs/fact-checker/post/how-many-pages-of-regulations-for-obamacare/2013/05/14/61eec914-bcf9-11e2-9b09-1638acc3942e_blog.html. Accessed November 29, 2022.
13. Cannan J. A legislative history of the Affordable Care Act: how legislative procedure shapes legislative history. *Law Libr J*. 2013;105(2):131–173. Available at: https://affordablecareactlitigation.files.wordpress.com/2018/09/llj_105n2_cannan.pdf. Accessed November 29, 2022.
14. Gluck AR, Regan M, Turret E. The Affordable Care Act's litigation decade. *Georgetown Law J*. 2020;108(6):1471–1534. Available at: https://www.law.georgetown.edu/georgetown-law-journal/in-print/volume-108/volume-108-issue-6-june-2020/the-affordable-care-acts-litigation-decade. Accessed May 3, 2023.
15. Rostron A. The Dickey Amendment on federal funding for research on gun violence: a legal dissection. *Am J Public Health*. 2018;108(7):865–867. Available at: https://ajph.aphapublications.org/doi/full/10.2105/AJPH.2018.304450. Accessed November 29, 2022.
16. Tung GJ, Vernick JS, Stuart EA, Webdter DW, Gielen AC. Federal actions to incentivise state adoption of 0.08 g/dL blood alcohol concentration laws. *Inj Prev*. 2017;23(5):309–313. Available at: http://dx.doi.org/10.1136/injuryprev-2016-042087. Accessed November 29, 2022.
17. Hourihan M. The federal budget process 101. American Association for the Advancement of Science. July 15, 2014. Available at: https://www.aaas.org/news/federal-budget-process-101-0. Accessed November 13, 2022.
18. Henderson C. Letter to Mayor Bowser on requiring vaccination against COVID-19. Council of the District of Columbia. August 24, 2021. Available at: https://www.christinahendersondc.com/press-releases/letter-to-mayor-bowser-require-vaccination-against-covid-19-for-all-public-school-employees-child-care-facility-employees-and-dc-government-connected-individuals-who-have-regular-contact-with-minors. Accessed November 29, 2022.
19. HHS Organizational Charts Office of Secretary and Divisions. US Department of Health and Human Services. Available at: https://www.hhs.gov/about/agencies/orgchart/index.html. Accessed January 4, 2023.
20. Institute of Medicine (US) Committee on Improving the Organization of the US Department of Health and Human Services (HHS) to Advance the Health of Our Population. HHS in the 21st century: charting a new course for a healthier America. National Academies Press. 2009. Available at: https://www.ncbi.nlm.nih.gov/books/NBK215021/?report=reader. Accessed November 13, 2022.
21. Bunk A. Federal register 101. *Proceedings*. 2010;67(1):55–57. Available at: https://www.federalregister.gov/uploads/2011/01/fr_101.pdf. Accessed November 13, 2022.

22. Department of Health and Human Services. How to participate in the rulemaking process. Available at: https://www.hhs.gov/sites/default/files/regulations/rulemaking-tool-kit.pdf. Accessed November 13, 2022.
23. Person C. ASTHO profile survey of state and territorial public health, United States, 2019 (ICPSR 37996) V2. Health & Medical Care Archive. 2022. Available at: https://doi.org/10.3886/ICPSR37996.v2. Accessed November 13, 2022.
24. Charles Evans Hughes. Columbia 250. Available at: http://c250.columbia.edu/c250_celebrates/remarkable_columbians/charles_hughes.html. Accessed November 13, 2022.
25. Hamilton A. The federalist papers: no. 78. The Avalon Project: Documents in Law, History and Diplomacy. Available at: https://avalon.law.yale.edu/18th_century/fed78.asp. Accessed November 13, 2022.
26. MacDowall L, Ackie M, Chapman R. Federal court strikes down Dallas paid sick leave ordinance. Littler. April 2, 2021. Available at: https://www.littler.com/publication-press/publication/federal-court-strikes-down-dallas-paid-sick-leave-ordinance. Accessed February 7, 2023.
27. de Beaumont Foundation, Kaiser Permanente. 2021 policy assessment. CityHealth. Available at: https://www.cityhealth.org/wp-content/uploads/2021/12/CH_POLICY-ASSESSMENT_2021.pdf. Accessed February 7, 2023.

Appendix 2A: US Department of Health and Human Services Operating Divisions

The US Department of Health and Human Services (HHS) has 11 operating divisions, including 8 agencies in the US Public Health Service and 3 human services agencies. These divisions administer a wide variety of health and human services and conduct life-saving research for the nation, protecting and serving all Americans.

US PUBLIC HEALTH SERVICE AGENCIES

Agency for Healthcare Research and Quality (AHRQ): Funds and conducts health services research to examine how people get access to care, how much care costs, and what happens to patients as a result the of care they receive. Information from AHRQ's research is used to assist consumers and health care providers in making more informed decisions and in improving the quality of health care services nationwide. For further information, visit: https://www.ahrq.gov.

Agency for Toxic Substances and Disease Registry (ATSDR): Investigates environmental exposures to hazardous substances in communities and takes action to reduce harmful exposures and their health consequences. ATSDR efforts prevent exposure to such substances, adverse human health effects, and diminished quality of life associated with exposure to hazardous substances. For further information, visit: https://www.atsdr.cdc.gov.

Centers for Disease Control and Prevention (CDC): Protects the public health as the federal government's lead public health agency by providing leadership and direction in the prevention and control of diseases and other preventable conditions, and by responding to public health emergencies. CDC collaborates to create the expertise, information, and tools that people and communities need to protect their health through health promotion, prevention of disease, injury and disability, and preparedness for new health threats. For further information, visit: https://www.cdc.gov.

US Food and Drug Administration (FDA): Ensures that food is safe, pure, and wholesome; ensures that human and animal drugs, biological products, and medical devices are safe and effective; and that electronic products that emit radiation are safe. FDA also has the responsibility to reduce death and disease caused by tobacco by regulating the manufacturing, marketing, and distribution of tobacco products and by educating the public about the harms of tobacco products to prevent initiation and encourage cessation. For further information, visit: https://www.fda.gov.

Health Resources and Services Administration (HRSA): Provides equitable health care to people who are geographically isolated and economically or medically vulnerable, including people with HIV, pregnant people, mothers and their families, those with low incomes, residents of rural areas, American Indians and Alaska Natives, and those otherwise unable to access high quality health care. HRSA programs also support health infrastructure, including through training of health professionals and distributing them to areas where they are needed most, providing financial support to health care providers, and advancing telehealth. For further information, visit: https://www.hrsa.gov.

Indian Health Service (IHS): Provides comprehensive health services for American Indians and Alaska Natives. IHS also offers an opportunity for maximum tribal involvement in developing and managing programs to improve their health status and overall quality of life. https://www.ihs.gov.

National Institutes of Health (NIH): Through its 27 institutes and centers, NIH supports and conducts research, domestically and abroad, into the causes, diagnosis, treatment, control, and prevention of diseases. It also promotes the acquisition and dissemination of medical knowledge to health professionals and the public. For further information, visit: https://www.nih.gov.

Substance Abuse and Mental Health Services Administration (SAMHSA): Improves access and reduces barriers to high quality, effective programs and services for individuals who suffer from or are at risk for addictive and mental disorders, as well as for their families and communities. SAMHSA also helps to ensure dollars are invested in evidence-based and data-driven programs and initiatives that result in improved health and resilience. For further information, visit: https://www.samhsa.gov.

HUMAN SERVICES AGENCIES

Administration for Children and Families (ACF): Promotes the economic and social well-being of families, children, individuals, and communities through a range of educational and supportive programs in partnership with states, tribes, and community organizations. ACF grant programs lead the nation in strengthening economic independence and productivity and in enhancing quality of life for people across their life span. For further information, visit: https://www.acf.hhs.gov.

Administration for Community Living (ACL): Increases access to community support and resources for the unique needs of older Americans and people with disabilities. The ACL includes the efforts and achievements of the Administration on Aging, the Office on Disability, and the Administration on Intellectual and Developmental Disabilities in a single agency, with enhanced policy and program support for both crosscutting initiatives and efforts focused on the unique needs of individual groups, such as children with developmental disabilities, adults with physical disabilities, and seniors, including seniors with Alzheimer's disease and related dementias. For further information, visit: https://acl.gov.

Centers for Medicare and Medicaid Services (CMS): The largest purchaser of health care in the United States, providing health coverage for more than 100 million individuals through the administration of Medicare, Medicaid, the Children's Health Insurance Program (CHIP), and new private insurance and private insurance market reform programs. For further information, visit: https://www.cms.gov.

3

Five Guiding Principles to Policy Engagement

In the previous chapters, we provided an overview of what policy is and where it happens. You are almost ready to dive in. But first, we want to pass along five insider tips that every public health practitioner should know before actively engaging in the policymaking process. Think of these as grounding principles. While not exhaustive, we hope these truths offer a useful framework to help prepare and inspire you to take action.

- Policymaking is messy.
- How you engage is personal.
- "Lobbying" is not a dirty word.
- Your message should align with your target audience.
- Policymaking takes a village.

POLICYMAKING IS MESSY

Let's disabuse ourselves of any notion that the process toward sound policy will be neat, tidy, and linear. The fact is, policymaking is a cyclical, iterative process that is filled with fits and starts, and it can often be messy. In fact, sometimes it can be very messy. While the road ahead may be long and winding, the work is necessary to bring about transformative change.

The history of the Tobacco 21 (T21) movement provides a clear example of the fits and starts that, while most certainly challenging to navigate, nevertheless yielded incredible health benefits. Tobacco remains the leading cause of preventable disease and death in the United States.[1] T21 is a policy aimed at raising the minimum legal age to purchase tobacco and nicotine products from 18 to 21. In its earliest days, this policy was divisive despite the well-documented long-term health implications of youth initiation on overall health outcomes. Due to a well-resourced tobacco industry with a long history of predatory practices, curbing tobacco-related harms has been and continues to be an uphill battle.

The T21 movement started in earnest in Needham, Massachusetts. Needham became the first town in the country to raise the minimum legal sales age for tobacco and nicotine products to 21 in February 2003.[2] The passage of this law heralded the emergence of a nationwide movement to increase the sales age, but T21 did not become the law of the land until it was federally passed in December 2019. For those of you doing the math, that's 16 years of continuous advocacy in cities, towns, and states across the country before a federal policy change was realized. The effort was extensive, and the strategies took many forms over the years, but the work highlights the significant role of policy and public health advocacy to better control and regulate tobacco usage. The ultimate lesson here is persistence. No matter how long the fight, no matter the twists and turns, constant, committed engagement is key. Stay the course.

HOW YOU ENGAGE IS PERSONAL

The policymaking process provides several critical opportunities for public health practitioners, researchers, communities, and other stakeholders to inform policy. Your role can, and likely should, take many forms, from providing recommendations or working on the inside as a staffer or champion to engaging the community or collaborating with partner organizations. These options are discussed in detail in Chapter 6. Choosing to engage in the policymaking process, whether through direct advocacy, providing written testimony during a hearing, or supporting your professional organization's policy efforts, is very much a personal decision (see Box 3-1). There is no wrong choice, and all forms of engagement are needed.

"LOBBYING" IS NOT A DIRTY WORD

On the healthcare side, lobbying is routinely conducted to help advance causes. Research America worked closely with universities across the country, tapping their own lobbying operations, along with academic and pharmaceutical government affairs teams, to help double the National Institutes of Health budgets. Unfortunately, as quantified in the Health Affairs article, *Public Health Needs Stronger Lobbying*, "Public health organizations

---

Box 3-1. Activism, Advocacy, and Everything in Between

> Following the August 2014 shooting and death of teenager Mike Brown at the hands of a Ferguson, Missouri, police officer, I was angry. At the time, I was working as a legislative staffer for the DC Council, and I didn't know what I could do. I was sick and tired of being sick and tired and knew I needed to do something. Days later, I joined others in shared outrage on a 13-hour bus trip to Ferguson to protest police brutality. The decision to engage in civil disobedience is one I've made many times throughout my life, and each time it was for deeply personal reasons. There are a myriad of ways that public health practitioners can engage, and each avenue is valid, important, and necessary, so choose what works for you.
>
> –Katrina S. Forrest, JD

spend pennies on lobbying compared to other health-related professions and associations, an imbalance that may perpetuate the system's problems."[3]

For many historical and contextual reasons, public health organizations often fear, frown upon, or actively avoid lobbying. This is especially true for those operating within governmental public health, where there are more strict regulations and restrictions on lobbying than for those working in the private sector. The nonprofit sector falls in between, with lobbying restrictions on governmental and private foundation funds. However, there is a lot of opportunity to engage in policymaker education, outreach, and varying rules for lobbying. Public health practitioners are often trained as researchers, scientists, and guardians of evidence, roles typically regarded as impartial and nonpartisan. But while the word "lobbying" or the idea of a lobbyist may conjure images of unsavory characters behaving in duplicitous ways, lobbying is a legal and critically important lever for policy change.

The First Amendment of the Constitution states

> Congress shall make no law respecting an establishment of religion, or prohibiting the free exercise thereof; or abridging the freedom of speech, or of the press; or the right of the people peaceably to assemble, and to petition the Government for a redress of grievances.[4]

While "lobby" is not a term expressly stated in the Constitution, the last sentence of the First Amendment, "to petition the Government for a redress of grievances," is modernly read as a right to lobby.

Lobbying is regulated through various federal, state, and local statutes and regulations, but, broadly speaking, the Federal Regulation of Lobbying Act of 1946 was first enacted to provide members of Congress with key information about those that lobby them. This law was eventually replaced by the Lobbying Disclosure Act of 1995, which was substantially amended by the Honest Leadership and Open Government Act of 2007. Together, these laws are designed to strengthen accountability in federal lobbying practices, enhance public disclosure requirements around lobbying activity and funding, and restrict gifts to members of Congress and their staff, among other things.

Why does this matter? Because, whether right or wrong, lobbying carries with it a negative perception, which "breeds visceral animosity and unfairly paints lobbying as undemocratic and inherently corrupt."[5] This view is enhanced when people see health organizations using lobbying for self-interest rather than the common good. For instance, the American Medical Association has lobbied[6] against universal health coverage since 1948,[7] and the American Hospital Association spent considerable lobbying dollars against Congressional bills to halt surprise medical billing.[3,8]

Lobbying is an integral part of a participatory government and provides another avenue to influence policies to ensure that they prioritize health and wellness. In addition, many important activities, such as policymaker education and invited testimony, do not

Direct Lobbying

Communication directly to a legislator, legislative branch staffer, or to an executive branch official or staff involved in formulating the legislation

Reflects a view on specific legislation
Legislation includes but is not limited to:
- Bills that have been introduced
- Specific legislative proposals not yet introduced
- Budget bills

Grassroots Lobbying

Communication to the public (e.g., speeches, advertisements, op-eds)

Reflects a view on specific legislation
and **includes a call-to-action**
The call-to-action does one of the following:
- Asks audience to contact a legislator
- Identifies a legislator as being the audience's representative;
- Provides contact information for a legislator;
- Identifies a legislator's position on the legislation as being undecided or opposing the communication's viewpoint;
- Identifies a legislator as sitting on the voting committee; or
- Provides a vehicle for contacting the legislation (e.g., form email, petition).

Source: Based on National Association for the Education of Young Children.[9]

Figure 3-1. Direct Lobbying and Grassroots Lobbying

qualify as lobbying. Therefore, understanding the legal framework of lobbying is critically important. By understanding what is and isn't lobbying, you can more effectively engage in discussions with policymakers.

Simply put, lobbying is any attempt to influence key governmental decisions or actions. According to the Internal Revenue Service, there are different forms of lobbying, which have different restrictions. As described in Figure 3-1, direct lobbying involves directly communicating with a member of the legislative body or other government official.[9] In comparison, grassroots lobbying involves mobilizing the general public to contact governmental officials about a particular issue. As a general rule, government funds and funds deriving from charitable foundations cannot be used for lobbying. This guidance is not intended to serve as legal advice, and there are exceptions to these general rules. When in doubt, check with legal counsel. Always understand the parameters of lobbying applicable to you or your respective organization to determine the right approach.

YOUR MESSAGE SHOULD ALIGN WITH YOUR TARGET AUDIENCE

Whether you choose to provide verbal or written testimony or some other tactic, you should have a clear message that aligns with your target audience. As discussed in Chapter 4, how you engage with executive leadership will be different from how you engage with legislative leadership. Your message should be tailored to ensure that it resonates and can be received by the audience you are seeking to influence.

Understanding message alignment starts with listening to and understanding your target audience(s). How do they speak on the issues you care about? What framing do they use? What words do they avoid? Each audience will have a different view of your issue and will require different information to make sense of, prioritize, and ultimately support your efforts (see Box 3-2).

In de Beaumont Foundation's latest book, *Talking Health: A New Way to Communicate About Public Health*, the importance of effective communication is explained in this way:

> Communication skills have been a consistent challenge for public health practitioners. In 2015, Katherine Lyon Daniel, then the associate director of communication at the CDC, suggested that "public health" may be a "dirty word" to people not in the field. She referenced a CDC Foundation study that found the term "public health" tested poorly among nonpublic health professionals. "If we keep talking to people in the same words that we want to use," she said, "then we're not going to be understood. . . . We have to adapt."[10(p3–4)]

Box 3-2. Telling Your Stories Matters in Policymaking

Early in my career, I conducted health assessments of hazardous waste sites for New Jersey's environmental agency. It was a rudimentary job, low in the bureaucratic hierarchy. Never in my wildest dreams had I imagined appearing before the US House of Representatives. Congress was debating cutting the SuperFund law that supported cleanup of the most toxic sites. APHA tapped me to provide insights on community risks. Despite being a state employee funded with federal dollars, my invited testimony was not considered lobbying. By the time I spoke, lawmakers were tired, bored, and distracted. I opened with a vivid telling of my experience investigating a fenced-off, low-priority site, only to find that it had been secretly transformed into a dirt-park playground like something out of a sci-fi movie. Children splashed in iridescent water pools saturated with dangerous chemicals. The story captured unexpected realities of human exposures at hazardous waste sites and emphasized the importance of continuing remediation. The program was not cut, and legislators from both sides of the aisle asked for follow-up meetings. I learned quickly that true stories from the front lines of public health can make a difference.

–Shelley Hearne, DrPH, MPH

Note: APHA = American Public Health Association.

In other words, public health practitioners cannot continue to rely on the jargon of the field or continue to operate within their own echo chambers. If we are going to move the needle on policy, we have to tailor our messages so they are heard, easily understood, and compelling.

A good example of framing is the successful effort to advance health equity policies in urban settings all across America. CityHealth, an initiative of de Beaumont Foundation and Kaiser Permanente, works to advance and promote a package of tried and tested policy solutions in the nation's 75 largest cities. Given the differences between cities like New York, Chicago, or Los Angeles, and Greensboro, Toledo, or Lincoln, CityHealth has worked to identify ways to customize their messages for both conservative and progressive audiences. Words like "policy" may be off-putting to some audiences, where "solution" may be more palatable. Similarly, CityHealth has learned that its annual assessment does not resonate as much with conservative audiences as "annual progress review." On a similar note, when engaged in local level policy work, issues around preemption are inevitable. However, the word "preemption" alone tends to stymie conversations before they even start, whereas the phrase "structural issues" provides just enough specificity to make the point clear while remaining ambiguous enough to invite continued discussion. These language adjustments may seem like a game of semantics, but they can be the difference between solidifying relationships and inadvertently alienating prospective allies.

POLICYMAKING TAKES A VILLAGE

Before ever engaging with policymakers, you must first answer two important questions: (1) What public health problem am I trying to solve, and (2) who am I working with to solve it? The answer to these questions unlocks everything and allows you to play an effective role in setting the policy agenda.

There are numerous political science models that map out how a governmental policy becomes a priority and gets put into action.[11,12] Fundamentally, these frameworks suggest that policies are most likely to become a reality when three conditions are present: (1) convergence of attention to the problem, (2) feasible and credible policy options, and (3) opportune political dynamics, such as a supportive society, organized constituencies, and aligned governmental entities. John Kingdon highlights that the problem, the policy, and political streams must come together in order to create a window for action.[12] Public health solutions and recommendations have the best chance for success when formed with an understanding of the political realities of policymaking.

Kingdon's agenda setting model emphasizes that people are critical of making policy change happen. Communities, in particular, have a crucial role to play in holding policymakers accountable and in partnering with public health to develop and assess policy solutions. The more we collaborate and coordinate with communities, the more effective we can be in the policymaking process. We define *communities* broadly to include people in a physical space with each other and people who share common interests, backgrounds, and identities. We also recognize that people are part of multiple communities. Iton and colleagues define *community power* as:

> The ability of people facing similar circumstances to develop, sustain, and grow an organized base of people who act together through democratic structures to set agendas, shift public discourse, influence who makes decisions, and cultivate ongoing relationships of mutual accountability with decision-makers that change systems and advance health equity.[13]

The power of the people is essential for formulating and implementing policies that are equitable and informed by the lived experiences of those in communities. When considering who to work with, it is important to think broadly and creatively. Public health is intertwined with many sectors; thus, it is difficult to imagine solving a public health problem without closely collaborating with other sectors. Multisector or cross-sector collaborations can help bring people and organizations together to maximize the resources, capacity, and energy available to tackle complex problems, like climate change and gun violence. In an article on cross-sector collaborations, Becker and Smith said, "Complex challenges are often approached through siloed solutions.... But rarely are these attempts sufficient because the challenges we face are the result not of one policy, investment, or program, but of the interactions between them."[14] Because of these interactions, the public health sector needs to work with housing, transportation, energy, public safety, and other sectors to solve complex problems. The public health sector can bring valuable skills, knowledge, and expertise that other sectors don't have to the table.

As you prepare to fully immerse yourself in the policy engagement process, we hope these grounding principles offer some foundational insights to quell fears or apprehension, spark new curiosity, and ultimately motivate you to take action.

Key Takeaways

- Policymaking is messy, so persistence and constant, committed engagement are key.
- How you engage in the policymaking process is very much a personal decision, and all types of engagement are needed.
- Do not be scared of lobbying. Just understand the rules so you can be more effective engaging in discussions with policymakers.
- Tailor your message to ensure that it resonates and can be received by the audience you are seeking to influence.
- Answer this important question before engaging with policymakers: what public health problem am I trying to solve and who am I working with to solve it?

REFERENCES

1. Centers for Disease Control and Prevention. Fast facts and fact sheets: smoking and cigarettes. August 22, 2022. Available at: https://www.cdc.gov/tobacco/data_statistics/fact_sheets/fast_facts/index.htm. Accessed January 2, 2023.
2. Reynolds MJ, Crane R, Winickoff JP. The emergence of the Tobacco 21 movement from Needham, Massachusetts, to throughout the United States (2003–2019). *Am J Public Health*. 2019;109(11):1540–1547. Available at: https://doi.org/10.2105/AJPH.2019.305209. Accessed November 13, 2022.
3. Coles E, Krasna H. Public health needs stronger lobbying. *Health Affairs Forefront*. September 1, 2022. Available at: https://www.healthaffairs.org/content/forefront/public-health-needs-stronger-lobbying. Accessed November 13, 2022.
4. US CONST amend I.
5. Allard NW. The seven deadly virtues of lobbyists: what lawyer lobbyists really do. *Elect Law J*. 2014;13(1):210–219. Available at: https://brooklynworks.brooklaw.edu/cgi/viewcontent.cgi?article=1532&context=faculty. Accessed November 13, 2022.
6. American Medical Association. AMA vision on health care reform. 2023. Available at: https://www.ama-assn.org/delivering-care/patient-support-advocacy/ama-vision-health-care-reform#:~:text=The%20AMA%20has%20long%20advocated,and%20universal%20access%20for%20patients. Accessed February 2, 2023.
7. Lepore J. The lie factory. *New Yorker*. September 17, 2012. Available at: https://www.newyorker.com/magazine/2012/09/24/the-lie-factory. Accessed February 2, 2023.
8. American Hospital Association. AHA, AMA and others file lawsuit over No Surprises Act rule that jeopardizes access to care. December 9, 2021. Available at: https://www.aha.org/news/news/2021-12-09-aha-ama-and-others-file-lawsuit-over-no-surprises-act-rule-jeopardizes-access. Accessed February 2, 2023.
9. National Association for the Education of Young Children. Rules of 501(c)(3) nonprofit lobbying. Available at: https://www.naeyc.org/our-work/public-policy-advocacy/rules-501c3-nonprofit-lobbying. Accessed November 13, 2022.
10. Miller MR, Castrucci BC, Locke R, Haskins J, Castillo GA, eds. *Talking Health: A New Way to Communicate About Public Health*. Oxford, UK: Oxford University Press; 2022.
11. Shiffman J. Agenda setting in public health. In: Quah SR, ed. *International Encyclopedia of Public Health*. 2nd ed. Cambridge, MA: Academic Press; 2017:16–21.
12. Kingdon JW. *Agendas, Alternatives, and Public Policies: Updated Edition With an Epilogue on Health Care*. 2nd ed. London, UK: Pearson; 2011.
13. Iton A, Ross RK, Tamber PS. Building community power to dismantle policy-based structural inequity in population health. *Health Aff*. 2022;41(12). Available at: https://doi.org/10.1377/hlthaff.2022.00540. Accessed January 2, 2023.
14. Smith DB, Becker, J. The essential skills of cross sector leadership. *Stanf Soc Innov Rev*. 2017;16(1):C4–C6. Available at: https://doi.org/10.48558/T176-EB11. Accessed January 2, 2023.

4

The Policymakers: What Do They Need to Make Good Public Health Decisions?

DECISION-MAKERS ARE PEOPLE, TOO.

For all the pomp and circumstance surrounding appointed and elected decision-makers, it's important to remember that they are people too. We all inhabit multiple identities. Whether someone is a senator, attorney, and mother or a mayor, musician, and part-time astrologer, all of our identities exist within us and surface or recede depending on the circumstances. Before engaging with decision-makers, it is critical to understand who they are and what motivates them. Like us, their perceptions, choices, and actions are often influenced by and executed in accordance with the identity that is most prominent for them at a specific moment in time. Still, identity is only one factor driving decision-making. In this chapter, we will also explore the roles of intrinsic and extrinsic motivations as we aim to demystify our target audiences and understand their needs.

For the purpose of this book, *decision-makers* is a broad term encompassing any person with the power and authority to influence or determine actions, policies, and practices at the federal, state, or local level. Figure 4-1 highlights several different decision-makers and their respective roles. Let this serve as a reminder that diverse decision-makers operate in specific ways and play unique functions.

One of the cornerstones of effective policy engagement is understanding the target audience. This means that public health practitioners should avoid a one-size-fits-all approach and instead be intentional in developing an engagement plan that balances the nuances of distinct groups. Customizing your approach is critical for reaching your intended audience.

Building an enabling environment for policy change requires an analysis of those in power. Whom do you aim to convince, legislators or executive department administrators? What motivates that decision-maker? Have they championed other issues that closely align with the policy change you seek? Answers to these questions will help public health practitioners home in on their core audience and determine how to design messages and materials that compel action.

At the beginning of the chapter, we discussed the role that identity plays in influencing our actions and how we navigate the world. Far too often, we hold our decision-makers to impossible standards, but the truth is that decision-makers are subject to the same cognitive and behavioral limitations as the rest of us.

Federal and state government agencies
These agencies often design and issue regulations and reporting requirements.

Legislators
This group includes elected federal, state, and local representatives (such as mayors and state representatives) who pass laws and oversee the public budget.

Public officials and administrators
This group includes people who administer budgets and generally lead or coordinate the implementation of the policy. An example is the director of a state's Medicaid program.

State and local board members
This group includes members of boards of health and planning and zoning committees.

Figure 4-1. Decision-Makers

Political scientists Paul Cairney and Richard Kwiatkowski explain it this way:

People use shortcuts to gather enough information to make decisions quickly: the 'rational', by pursuing clear goals and prioritising certain kinds of information, and the 'irrational', by drawing on emotions, gut feelings, values, beliefs, habits, and the familiar, to make decisions quickly.... policymakers face unusually strong and constant pressures on their cognition and emotion.... Perhaps their solutions seem to be driven more by their values and emotions than a 'rational' analysis of the evidence, often because we hold them to an information processing standard that no human being can reach.[1(p2)]

If we are to inspire action and drive lasting policy change, we must first see decision-makers as *people*, fallible beings that are processing the world and the endless information cycle in ways that are not that dissimilar to our own.

To understand how a decision-maker might analyze a problem, we must pay close attention to how they identify. Do they consider themselves conservative or progressive? Are they a parent? Are they an advocate for business innovation? How might their racial identity inform their decisions? Have those identities factored into their responses? While it may be challenging to cement a causal connection, recognizing that choices are often identity-based is vital to determining when and how to engage with a decision-maker.

Various situations and circumstances in the world around us can trigger or affirm different aspects of our identities, leading to a specific action or outcome. A politician, for example, may vote to support a bill advanced by their party solely because of their membership in said party. David Broockman explains that "politicians are reliably more likely to advance the interests of those who share their personal characteristics, including their gender, race, profession, class, and sexual orientation."[2(p521)] Understanding the underlying motivations of decision-makers is critical to understanding what positions they may take in response to an issue. This understanding can help determine how they may hear and perceive information. It can help predict how they may react or respond to policy proposals and, ultimately, how they will vote on the issues we care about.

In addition to identity, it is important to consider a decision-maker's intrinsic and extrinsic motivations. In politics, we have often heard the moniker "The People's Champion" used to gain support from likely voters. The goal is often to represent the candidate as a person who will speak, fight, and advocate on behalf of the community. Essentially, this is a way to play up a candidate's intrinsic motivations. Voters are to believe that this is a person motivated by a desire to serve, irrespective of the money or power they stand to gain. If a decision-maker is truly motivated by a genuine desire to do the best for the most people, public health practitioners can frame issues and situate solutions in a way that amplifies the expected outcomes and reach of a proposed intervention.

Extrinsic motivation is derived from external sources and expectations, such as a looming reelection, constituent feedback, accolades, or money. The Fight for $15 illustrates how strong, coordinated advocacy plays into the extrinsic motivations of elected officials to prioritize policy change. In 2012, hundreds of fast-food workers in New York City walked off the job in an effort to unionize workers and increase wages for fast-food employees across the city.[3] The federal minimum wage was last set at $7.25 per hour in 2009.[4] Unable to afford basic necessities, the fast-food workers in New York forged a movement, which came to be known as the Fight for $15. Thanks to targeted and consistent advocacy, the momentum brought on by the Fight for $15 compelled politicians to take decisive action, adopting a $15 minimum wage in several states and more than two dozen cities. President Joe Biden later campaigned to raise the federal minimum wage to $15 per hour, and in 2022 he signed an executive order doing just that for federal workers and contractors.[5] Though Congressional action is needed to accomplish a federal minimum wage of $15 per hour, the recent groundswell points toward similar actions at the state and local levels. This shows that collective action and constituency pressure are unquestionably effective tools.

Parsing out motivations as either intrinsic or extrinsic can be difficult. When analyzing voting patterns of congresspeople as it related to the Civil Rights Act of 1990, Brookman's research indicated that "legislators act more in line with their extrinsic incentives when they believe they are under great scrutiny, but that less scrutinized behavior reveals something about their true preferences."[2(p524)] In other words, consistent public pressure and the risk of heightened scrutiny are external factors that tend to spur the immediate action on the part of decision-makers. This is a finding that public health practitioners can and should use to their advantage.

Decision-makers, like us, are all motivated by something, whether it's identity or intrinsic and extrinsic factors. To understand the motivations of decision-makers, we must pay close attention. Public health practitioners should commit to watching hearings and listening to the types of questions being asked. We should regularly review voting records, read recent newsletters, engage on social media, pull daily news clips, and hold meetings with the right people. We need to understand whether decision-makers have taken previous actions that suggest they would be willing to act on public health issues. We need to ascertain our level of authority and identify the players in our social and political spheres of influence. Successful engagement is, in part, based on the work we put in at the outset to know and understand the decision-makers we seek to influence.

WHAT DO POLICYMAKERS NEED?

When you are ready to engage, it is important to ask yourself, what exactly do the decision-makers need? Figure 4-2 provides a general outline of five key things decision-makers will need to inform their decisions: evidence, context, clear and concise messaging, credible messengers, and timing (i.e., window of opportunity). Decision-makers cannot be expected to be experts on every issue. Public health practitioners are uniquely positioned to influence policy change through strong policy development, compelling storytelling, and effective engagement with decision-makers.

Evidence

Public health practitioners are trained to identify and evaluate problems, isolate root causes, and analyze complex data. Evidence and science are expected to be dispassionate and unbiased, but alone they are mere numbers and text on a page. In order to engage with decision-makers, particularly in a climate where facts are questioned, we must use data to tell a compelling story. Storytelling should aim to maintain the integrity of the facts while applying them in a manner that centers people first, succinctly articulates the issue, and recommends viable solutions.

Evidence
Use data to tell a compelling story.
Center people first, succinctly articulate the issue, and recommend a viable solution.

Context
Shape the narrative arc.
Inform the decision-maker of history, participants, and factors.

Clear and Concise Messaging
Know your ask.
Craft a message that is clear, consistent, concise, and memorable.

Credible Messengers
Enlist allies with a unique message/shared stake, close relationships with/trusted by decision-maker, and access to an organized network.

Timing
Know when the time is right.
Understand decision-maker priorities and the Overton Window.

Figure 4-2. Influencing Policymaker Decision-Making

How evidence is collected, organized, and interpreted depends on the question. As discussed earlier, part of knowing your target audience is understanding the problems they are grappling with, then taking that one step further to identify the data points that will resonate with them the most. Data not encompassed in a story may fail to inspire action or drive change.

Finally, while evidence is important, we must resist the urge to bombard decision-makers with copious amounts of data. How you select and frame the data to create a compelling story will make all the difference. We will touch on this later in the chapter.

CONTEXT

Decision-makers are required to think and act quickly, weighing the opinions, beliefs, and positions of diverse constituencies. To engage decision-makers on the issues of greatest importance to you, context is necessary, as it adds specificity and helps to create connection between the decision-maker and the issue you are championing. Providing adequate context can help focus and frame the issue and demonstrate your understanding of the landscape.

Decision-makers need to understand why a past policy failed or succeeded, who was involved in the decision-making process, and what enabling or confounding factors contributed to the final outcome. Context enables decision-makers to understand the full scope of an issue and how to promote better practices and avoid past missteps. In addition to contextual details about your specific issue, decision-makers need to understand the broader context. For example, what current events are happening in the world around them? How is the media portraying an issue? Figure 4-3 speaks to all of the contextual contours that impact decision-making.[6] In connecting these dots for the decision-makers, we are in a position to shape the narrative and inform their decision-making process.

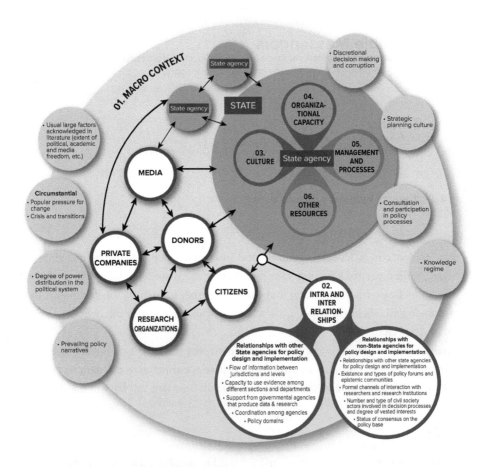

Source: Echt.[6] Reprinted with permission of Leandro Echt.

Figure 4-3. Context Matters

Contextual details can help decision-makers identify potential roadblocks and unearth the greatest potential for change/impact. However, beware of information overload and stick to the salient contextual points. Too much information can have the perverse effect of diluting or distorting your message.

Clear and Concise Messages

Part of being clear in your messaging is knowing what you ultimately want to achieve. What is your ask? As practitioners we must know what result we want, why we want it, and how we believe the result can be achieved. When it comes to policy engagement, being very clear about your ask is, perhaps, the single most critical aspect of the process because everything else is derived from it.

Once you have clarity and conviction around what you want, you can develop topline messages that leave an impression and build trust. As messengers of public health messages, we need to gain the trust of our audience and motivate them to act. They must strike the balance between presenting evidence and appealing to hearts and minds.

Additionally, the minutiae of the research methods will not hold the attention of policymakers. As discussed above, in sharing too much information, you run the risk of distorting or diluting your message. Ultimately, you want your message to sing. Think about the most annoying song you've ever heard and then the very moment you realize you can't get it out of your head! That's what we need in public health. We need our messages to leave an imprint long after we've made them, and we can do this by making our data and evidence more accessible, compelling, and concise. Decision-makers are inundated with information and, given the competing demands on their time, are more likely to take in messages that are memorable and straight to the point. If a recipient only has a few moments to hear your arguments, what is your pitch? All of your communications, especially your elevator speech, should be clear, consistent, and concise in how they articulate the policy problem, the solution, and its impacts (see Figure 4-4).[7]

Credible Messengers

How we assign meaning to what we hear is heavily dependent on the context in which we hear it or whom we hear it from. Knowing our audience also means identifying allies and partners that can help build an enabling environment for policy change. While a vocal mass can create power, amplify collective voices, and generate extrinsic motivation, it is important to be thoughtful and strategic when choosing allies. Engaging others on a topic simply for the sake of driving up numbers does a disservice to your goals. You should identify and enlist those allies who (1) have a unique perspective or a shared stake in the issue, (2) possess close relationships with the decision-makers you want to influence, (3) have access to an organized network around which to build a meaningful

An **elevator speech** is a message intended to spur decision-makers to action. It must be short, specific, and memorable. It is important to have your elevator speech rehearsed and ready because you never know when you'll have an opportunity to use it! Use the steps below to develop your elevator speech.

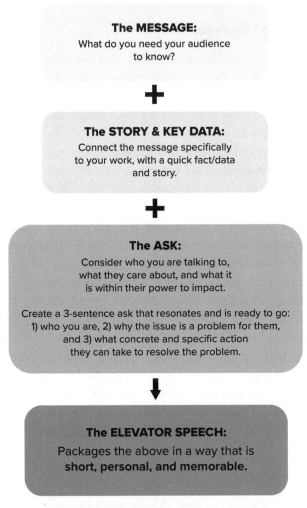

Source: American Library Association.[7] Adapted with permission.

Figure 4-4. Your Policymaker Elevator Speech

alliance, and/or (4) are credible and respected messengers whom the decision-makers trust (see Box 4-1).[8]

During the COVID-19 response, de Beaumont Foundation[9] completed a national poll, the results of which revealed that Americans trusted scientists and public health officials to deliver factual information. However, they felt that politicians were not

> **Box 4-1. Local Health Informing US Decision-Making**
>
> In 2016, Congress was mired in a debate about emergency funding for the emerging Zika virus. Texas Harris County Public Health (HCPH) invited Senator Cornyn, an influential Republican, to visit the local agency and learn about their innovative efforts in mosquito control. This gave Cornyn an opportunity to discuss Zika's risk to his constituents and the public health measures needed to prevent further spread. A few weeks after his visit, Congress passed a bill to provide $1.1 billion in funding for Zika. These types of on-the-ground engagements help provide perspective, build relationships, and connect the dots about how federal funds can be effectively used to improve and protect health.[8]

credible messengers about the pandemic. From this, we can speculate that at least some vaccine hesitancy may have been attributable to messengers that the public deemed untrustworthy. With all of the information learned in this chapter, public health practitioners must pull back and ask themselves, am I the right messenger to engage the decision-maker on this topic?

Timing

Timing is one of the most important variables when considering policymaker engagement, as it shapes the strategic opportunities available and influences the impact of your efforts. Think of timing in two discrete ways, the timing of the moment, which requires that you stay apprised of the landscape around you, and the timing for the future, which enables you to change the environment around you. As it relates to the former, most decision-makers, particularly elected officials, have a finite period of time in office. There is a limited window in which to realize their impact. For this reason, decision-makers act on and prioritize some policy issues and ignore others, whether intentionally or by circumstance. These priorities form the basis of a governmental policy agenda. Understanding which issues are top of mind for decision-makers can help you identify windows of opportunity and allow you to gauge momentum. This is why it is critical for you to keep a finger on the pulse of what is happening now. For example, budgets are policy documents, therefore it is imperative to understand the local, state, and federal budget cycles, as those hearings provide a recurrent, real-time opportunity to engage. Make sure to capitalize on these moments to get in front of elected leaders and advocate for your positions.

Additionally, it is critical to understand the power you wield to change the landscape around you. The Overton Window is a theory that helps us unpack policy priorities and political shifts over time. According to the Mackinac Center for Public Policy, the Overton Window is essentially the spectrum of policies and social issues that are deemed politically acceptable at a given moment in time.[10] Simply put, it's a model for understanding how ideas shift and change over time. It offers a window into the power of dynamic advocacy. Think about the living wage debate. There was a time when the notion of increased wages, particularly at the federal level, was so partisan and divisive that it remained at the fringes of public consciousness. However, as previously discussed, through the continued and sustained advocacy of coalitions across the country, attitudes shifted, creating new windows of opportunity and making the time ripe for policymaker engagement. So how far did attitudes shift? Well, in 2020, 60% of voters in Florida, a red state with two Republican senators, a Republican-controlled state legislature, and a Republican governor who all opposed a minimum wage increase at that time, approved a mandate to make the minimum wage $15 by 2026.[11,12] As advocates, even if the road ahead is long and arduous, you possess an immense ability to open new windows and create lasting change.

Timing is truly everything. Whether you seize the moments in front of you and capitalize on the current open policy windows or partner with other stakeholders for a sustained effort designed to open a window in the future, your success is heavily based on knowing just the right time to engage.

Key Takeaways

- Decision-makers are people, just like us. To be successful in our engagement with them, we must understand their identities, motivations, and priorities.
- To effectively influence decision-makers, it is important to approach them with evidence, context, clear and concise messaging, and credible messengers, and to know when the timing is right.
- Be prepared to make a clear and compelling ask. Ideally, the ask should be realistic, measurable, timely, and reflect the public and community's interest.
- Listen to and leverage the power of allies who may be better suited to deliver key messages.

REFERENCES

1. Cairney P, Kwiatkowski R. How to communicate effectively with policymakers: combine insights from psychology and policy studies. *Palgrave Commun*. 2017;3(37):1–8. Available at: https://doi.org/10.1057/s41599-017-0046-8. Accessed August 28, 2022.
2. Broockman DE. Black politicians are more intrinsically motivated to advance Blacks' interests: a field experiment manipulating political incentives. *Am J Pol Sci*. 2013;57(3):521–536. Available at: http://www.jstor.org/stable/23496636. Accessed August 28, 2022.
3. Greenhouse S. With day of protests, fast-food workers seek more pay. *New York Times*. November 29, 2012. Available at: https://www.nytimes.com/2012/11/30/nyregion/fast-food-workers-in-new-york-city-rally-for-higher-wages.html?auth=login-google1tap&login=google1tap. Accessed December 4, 2023.
4. Konish L. These states are raising their minimum wages in 2023. Chart shows where workers can expect higher pay. *CNBC*. January 1, 2023. Available at: https://www.cnbc.com/2023/01/01/these-states-will-raise-their-minimum-wages-in-2023.html#:~:text=As%20the%20calendar%20turns%20to%202023%2C%20workers%20in%20more%20than,the%20same%20rate%20since%202009. Accessed January 4, 2023.

5. Reinicke C. Biden's $15 minimum wage hike for federal agencies is now in effect. CNBC. January 21, 2022. Available at: https://www.cnbc.com/2022/01/21/bidens-15-minimum-wage-hike-for-federal-agencies-is-now-in-effect.html. Accessed February 2, 2023.
6. Echt L. "Context matters": a framework to help connect knowledge with policy in government institutions. London School of Economics and Political Science. December 28, 2017. Available at: https://blogs.lse.ac.uk/europpblog/2017/12/28/context-matters-a-framework-to-help-connect-knowledge-with-policy-in-government-institutions. Accessed November 18, 2022.
7. American Library Association. The elevator speech. Available at: https://www.ala.org/advocacy/advocacy-university/school-library-resources/elevator-speech. Accessed November 18, 2022.
8. Shah UA. Public health advocacy: informing lawmakers about what matters most in our communities. *Naccho Voice*. February 5, 2018. Available at: https://www.naccho.org/blog/articles/public-health-advocacy-informing-lawmakers-about-what-matters-most-in-our-communities. Accessed January 1, 2023.
9. Miller M. National poll reveals COVID-19 language to overcome political divide and save lives. de Beaumont Foundation. November 30, 2020. Available at: https://debeaumont.org/news/2020/poll-reveals-covid19-language-to-overcome-political-divide-and-save-lives. Accessed November 18, 2022.
10. Mackinac Center for Public Policy. The Overton Window. 2019. Available at: https://www.mackinac.org/OvertonWindow. Accessed November 18, 2022.
11. Pramuk J. Florida votes to raise state's minimum wage to $15 an hour. CNBC. Updated November 6, 2020. Available at: https://www.cnbc.com/2020/11/04/florida-votes-to-raise-minimum-wage-to-15-in-2020-election.html. Accessed February 8, 2023.
12. Kinder M. Even a divided America agrees on raising the minimum wage. Brookings Institution. November 13, 2020. Available at: https://www.brookings.edu/blog/the-avenue/2020/11/13/even-a-divided-america-agrees-on-raising-the-minimum-wage. Accessed February 8, 2023.

5

It Has to Be Fair and Inclusive: Approaching Policy With Equity in Mind

Now that you have insider knowledge on how to advance policies, how do you assure that they are fair and inclusive? One thing many people learned from the COVID-19 pandemic, which was not new to those in the public health field, is that some groups of people are more likely to contract diseases and die than others. This is a matter of *equity*, which refers to fairness and justice.[1] Equity is not the same as *equality* in that equality refers to treating everyone the same and giving each individual the same thing. Equity recognizes that everyone does not start from the same place and that we need to bring intention to rectifying these imbalances or inequities. Sometimes an approach to public health that centers equality makes sense. For example, giving all school-aged children in the District of Columbia a metro card so they can use public transit when they need to. But more often than not, issues of equity arise when we think about policy.

Equity is a key principle for effective policymaking, and we should intentionally approach policy change with equity in mind.[2] This is because policy change is one path to permanent social change; changing policies can help advance social justice and create long term systems reform. Policy can also help with the long-term work of shifting power by building power among communities that have been historically marginalized or oppressed, and by shifting power away from those who hold on to power to maintain inequitable power hierarchies.

In this chapter, we define equity and why it matters for policy, describe barriers to centering equity in the policy process, and provide tools that can help you center equity in the policy work that you do. Figure 5-1 includes definitions and key terms that will be introduced in this chapter.[3-5] Before diving in, we acknowledge that there is so much to be said regarding equity that we could write an entire book on the topic. Because we cannot do that here, we present an overview of the topic as it pertains to policy and offer resources if you want to learn more.

DEFINING EQUITY

Equity is fairness, plain and simple, and fairness means that everyone has the same opportunity to benefit. Because of this country's deep history characterized by colonialism, racism, and oppression, not all people living in the United States have the same opportunity to benefit. The COVID-19 pandemic illustrated just how clearly some people

Health Equity
means that everyone has a fair opportunity to be as healthy as possible.

Social Determinants of Health
refers to the political, economic, social, and physical drivers of health.

Structural Racism
refers "to the totality of ways in which societies foster racial discrimination through mutually reinforcing systems of housing, education, employment, earnings, benefits, credit, media, health care, and criminal justice. These patterns and practices in turn reinforce discriminatory beliefs, values, and distribution of resources." [2(p1453)]

Power
has many definitions, but when we use the term power, we are referring to the "capacity to do things to achieve a purpose." [3(p11)]

Multisector Collaborations
bring together the different sectors necessary to create, implement, and sustain successful strategies to achieve health equity.[4]

Source: Definitions from Bailey et al.,[3(p1453)] Healey et al.,[4(p11)] and National Academies of Sciences, Engineering, and Medicine et al.[5]

Figure 5-1. Key Concepts

have access to health care while others do not; how some people have access to paid sick leave and some do not; how some people can work from home and some cannot; how some families have access to childcare and private schools and some do not. The consequences of these inequities meant that Black, Latine, and Indigenous people, especially those with lower incomes and living in poverty, were more likely to contract the virus that causes COVID-19 and die from this preventable infectious disease than their white counterparts with more resources. It is important to note that COVID-19 is just one example of a health condition that disproportionately impacts certain communities because of deep-seeded, systemic inequities.

The lack of fairness or opportunity is closely tied to where an individual was born, grew up, and lives. In 2018, the National Center for Health Statistics released, for the first time, neighborhood-level data indicating how life expectancy estimates vary significantly by block.[6,7] The data, similar to many studies examining the influence of place on health, provides clear evidence that one's health is deeply tied to their city, town, neighborhood, and zip code. For example, where a child lives can dictate whether they go to a thriving school or a failing one. It dictates whether they have access to reliable, safe transportation or transit services that are inconsistent and unreliable, making a twenty-minute commute a two-hour one. A child's zip code or neighborhood can determine whether they will grow up in a neighborhood that is plagued by gun violence and an open-air drug market due to decades of disinvestment, which leads to a lack of opportunity for young people. These same neighborhoods also lack safe outdoor spaces for kids to play or grocery stores with healthy foods. Children in these neighborhoods are also more likely to be affected by environmental justice issues. This means they cannot play outside, even if they want to, because of poor air quality due to the presence of factories and highways that always seem to be built near low-income communities.

Innovative research conducted by Geographic Insights, an interdisciplinary research lab based at the Harvard Center for Population and Development Studies and the Harvard Center for Geographic Analysis, illustrate the differences in life expectancy by US congressional district level (see Figure 5-2).[8,9] This data shows not only the wide variation in life expectancy by geography, but also the opportunity to describe health outcomes in a way that resonates with members of Congress who have the power to implement federal health policies that could benefit the health of their constituents.

As explained in earlier chapters, the social determinants or drivers of health (SDOH) are closely tied to inequities in health. Healthy People 2030 defines *SDOH* as "the conditions in the environments where people are born, live, learn, work, play, worship, and age that affect a wide range of health, functioning, and quality-of-life outcomes and risks."[10] While there are several models of SDOH, the framework included in Healthy People 2030 groups them within five categories: economic stability, education access and quality, healthcare access and quality, neighborhood and built environment, and social and community context. Although the model does not specifically have a place for racism and discrimination, they are present in each of the areas and considered key SDOH. Drawing on the above description of the inequities tied to fairness, it is clear that SDOH are a significant contributor to inequities and health disparities that negatively impact certain racial and ethnic populations more than others.

ADVANCING HEALTH EQUITY THROUGH POLICY CHANGE

Because policy decisions have led to health inequities, it is important to acknowledge that policy decisions can also advance health equity so that everyone has a fair opportunity to be as healthy as possible. While the current state of the world may make it difficult to believe this is possible, we believe it is. Imagine if our country was one where your zip code didn't correlate strongly with your health status or where every single person,

58 | POLICY ENGAGEMENT

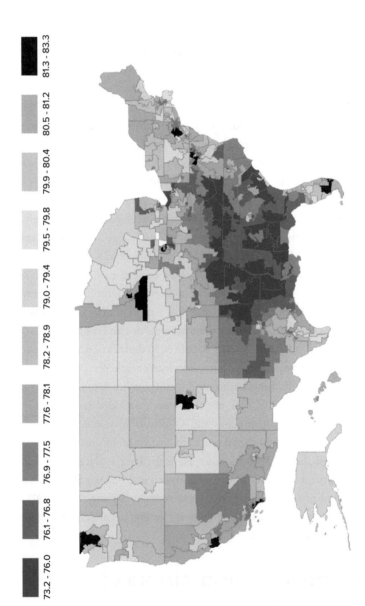

Source: Takai et al.[8] Adapted with permission of Elsevier and the Geographic Insights Lab, Harvard Center for Population and Development Studies and Elsevier.[9]
Note: Researchers at the Geographic Insights Lab at Harvard use geographic data for better evidence-based policymaking by providing members of Congress and their constituents with congressional district–level data that helps shape federal-level policies.

Figure 5-2. Life Expectancies at Birth Across Congressional Districts in the United States

> **Box 5-1. Connecting the Dots**
>
> Imagine a community that has no supermarket and lacks access to affordable and nutritious foods. We would say that lack of food access is a SDOH. Take the lack of a supermarket as an example. There are policies that could incentivize a supermarket to be built in a community. For example, Baltimore City offers personal property tax credit to supermarkets that are located in certain areas of the city that lack access to healthy food choices.[11] The role of policy in this scenario is considered a political determinant of health and health equity.

Note: SDOH = social determinant of health

regardless of their race, ethnicity, gender, sexual orientation, and immigration status, had the same opportunity to be healthy. What would it take to get there and why haven't we gotten there yet?

It is important to highlight that policies, and political forces, have played a major role in how SDOH such as housing, transportation, and education affect health (see Box 5-1).[11,12] The example mentioned earlier of legal discrimination in housing is one way this has played out in the United States.[12]

There is no easy answer as to why we have not prioritized health equity in the policy process, although there are several viable answers: (1) structural racism, (2) power imbalances, and (3) the deep siloes that characterize how our systems function. We briefly comment on each of these below.

Structural Racism

Many of the health inequities that exist today are the result of generations of oppressive policies rooted in structural racism. *Structural racism* refers "to the totality of ways in which societies foster racial discrimination through mutually reinforcing systems of housing, education, employment, earnings, benefits, credit, media, health care, and criminal justice. These patterns and practices in turn reinforce discriminatory beliefs, values, and distribution of resources."[3(p1453)] Structural racism is manifested in policies, practices, and programs in ways that segregate and prioritize populations based on race and ethnicity and create barriers to social opportunity and upward mobility. There are decades of research that indicate that these barriers drive marginalization and result in inequity in health and well-being among Black and Indigenous communities and other people of color.

Power

Advancing or achieving health equity and racial equity requires building community power to change policies and systems, and to dismantle structural inequities. Communities and individuals who are most impacted by structural inequities are often furthest away from formal centers of power.[13] Power has many definitions, but when we use the term *power*, we are referring to the "'capacity' to do things to 'achieve a purpose.'"[4(p1)] Structural racism and other systems of oppression in the United States have led to centuries of some populations exercising power over others and the resulting consequences of its imbalance. The result of this power imbalance has meant that certain populations have been prevented from the ability to obtain and build wealth and/or the ability to influence decisions, structures, and resource allocation. As a result, these communities have not reaped the health, material, or financial benefits equal to those in positions of power.

Thankfully, there has been a growing recognition within the field of public health and other related fields that building community power is central to promoting policy change that advances health equity.[14] This requires those in positions of power to share power with historically marginalized communities, and to do so in an authentic and caring way to avoid perpetuating harm. Shifting power requires that those in power commit to "widening—and ultimately shifting—the circle of people, communities, and networks making decisions and reprioritizing the problems and solutions to focus on."[15(p2)] Until there is a genuine commitment to shifting power by those who have power, efforts to advance health equity will not result in the structural changes that help communities, families, and individuals thrive. Audre Lorde once said, "The master's tools will never dismantle the master's house."[16] If inequities result in part from power imbalances, then we need to target those same power imbalances to eliminate inequities.

Multisector Collaborations

If it were easy to work across sectors, we would do it all the time. Siloes in local, state, and federal governments create barriers to working together, by which we mean really working together. Because of that, public health officials are highlighting multisector approaches, which is core to Public Health 3.0, an initiative launched by the US Department of Health and Human Services that focuses on intentional collaboration across health and nonhealth sectors.[17] These collaborations involve sectors working together to address complex problems and engage with communities that are historically marginalized and have been disproportionately harmed by poor health outcomes. Remember what was said earlier about power: effective collaborations across sectors, which also involve authentic community engagement, is one example of sharing power to create structural changes.

HOW TO ADVANCE EQUITABLE POLICIES

There are several tools that can be used during the policy process to intentionally consider health equity and racial equity. These tools include Health Impact Assessments (HIAs), health notes, and Racial Equity Impact Assessments (REIAs). These tools are designed to create a process by which the potential effects, benefits, and harms of a proposed policy are named and measured through various methods. The outcomes of the assessments, which show how health could be impacted if a certain proposal moves forward, are then shared with policymakers with the hope that they can make decisions that will not exacerbate existing inequities or harm health. These tools are being used to dismantle and address some of the policies, programs, and systems that have perpetuated inequities and contributed to disparities. When implemented effectively, they can be used to advance more equitable policies.

Health Impact Assessment

According to the National Research Council, an *HIA* is "a structured process that uses scientific data, professional expertise, and stakeholder input to identify and evaluate public health consequences of proposals and suggests pragmatic actions that could be taken to minimize adverse health impacts and optimize beneficial ones."[18(p3)] The HIA process is intended to be pragmatic in that it provides timely, useful judgments based on the best available knowledge and public health expertise. HIAs focus on solutions, offering feasible recommendations that can help minimize risks and maximize benefits.

Equity is a core value of the HIA process. HIAs examine potential health effects and the distribution of those effects within a population. They also focus on equity by involving an array of stakeholders at every step of the process, including community members who will be affected by a decision, policymakers, and others with an interest in the outcome. Evaluations of HIAs show that they help impacted populations and decision-makers weigh trade-offs and understand the direct and indirect health impacts of a proposal, as well as increase community capacity and address community concerns.[19,20]

According to the Pew Charitable Trusts cross-sector toolkit for health, there have been more than 400 HIAs completed or in process in the United States.[21] An example of an HIA that demonstrates how equity can be considered during the policy process is one related to a federal policy proposal that would impact the Supplemental Nutrition Assistance Program (SNAP). You would think that SNAP is a policy where the potential impacts on health and equity are clear. However, at a time when political actors were conscious of the dreaded "s" word (sequestration), Congress was focused on reducing spending by the Department of Agriculture, which meant that SNAP was negatively impacted. In fact, the HIA showed how proposed changes to SNAP benefits and eligibility would impact health, harm families and children, and exacerbate inequities. It also showed that these impacts would be costly. The team that conducted the HIA disseminated the findings directly to members of Congress, their staff, and relevant advocacy organizers. In short order, the data from the HIA were cited by one of the members during the debate about proposed changes to SNAP. Ultimately, the proposed cuts to SNAP were minimal because the proposed changes to SNAP eligibility never came to fruition.

Health Notes

HIAs are not always the right tool to bring health and equity to the policy process. To address this, a team at the Health Impact Project, a collaboration of the Robert Wood Johnson Foundation and the Pew Charitable Trusts, created and promoted a legislative health note.[22] A legislative *health note* provides brief, objective, and nonpartisan summaries of how proposed legislation could affect health. The analysis draws on the best available published research and public health expertise to help legislators understand the connections between their decisions and the health of their constituents. Health notes describe positive and negative effects on health and include available local data to amplify how the bill could impact specific populations by race, ethnicity, gender, and ability. They have also been applied to sectors outside of health and health care, such as education and employment, where policies can have profound impacts on shaping health and inequities. Similarly, they have been applied to bills covering various topics and sectors, including unemployment insurance changes, state funding for full-day kindergarten, and drug-sentencing reform.

Racial Equity Impact Assessments

A third tool, REIA, aims to address racial equity during policy formulation. One of the most robust efforts to promote REIAs is occurring in Washington, DC. The DC Council Office of Racial Equity (CORE) was charged with conducting REIAs on almost every piece of legislation proposed by the DC City Council. CORE defines *REIAs* as a "careful and organized examination of how a proposed bill will affect different racial and ethnic groups in the District of Columbia."[23] The analysis examines a bill's potential impact on residents of color and concludes whether the bill will likely make progress toward racial equity (i.e., the elimination of racial disparities), maintain the status quo, harm or improve outcomes, or have a negligible impact. When data are mixed or limited, an REIA may conclude that the impact on racial equity is inconclusive. REIAs are publicly available on the CORE website. They have already addressed a number of policies, including those related to labor, housing, transportation, education, human services, and government operations.[24]

Findings from HIAs, health notes, and REIAs have been shared during legislative testimony, which is one way to intentionally bring considerations about racial equity and health equity to the policy process.

CHALLENGES

We need leaders who understand equity, are committed to achieving health equity, and understand how to center equity in public health policies. This is where politics becomes an important part of the story. As noted in the book introduction, politics are a reality of the policymaking process. Public health professionals can identify policy champions who care about health equity and racial equity and make sure they are aware of these tools and their impact.

Even when there is political will, sometimes data limitations prohibit the effective use of the tools described in this section. For example, how many times do we see data reports with "other" listed as a race category or for "Black" people as if they are a monolithic population? In order to truly address inequities, we need to accurately describe the differences we want to address. That means collecting data with adequate specificity so the data is useful and can effectively inform equitable policies.

On January 20, 2021, the first day of the Biden-Harris Administration, President Biden signed an Executive Order (13985), Advancing Racial Equity and Support for Underserved Communities Through the Federal Government, which affirmed the role of the government in "advancing equity, civil rights, racial justice, and equal opportunity for all."[25] We have seen how this executive order has propelled various federal agencies to explicitly name equity goals, including creating Federal Equity Action Plans. The potential for advancing equity via federal policies is significant. This executive order is one example of how leadership can signal their commitment to advancing equity throughout an organization, in this case, the federal government.

Key Takeaways
- Equity is about fairness and justice. It recognizes that everyone does not start from the same place. Equity should be a key consideration in the policy process.
- Policy change is one path to permanent social change. Changing policies can help advance social justice and create long-term systems reform, as well as help with the long-term work of shifting power.
- Approaching policymaking with attention to equity means committing to equity during the policymaking process and when evaluating the potential policy outcomes.
- If we are intentional in ensuring that the policies we formulate and implement center equity and address the root causes and structures that contribute to health and racial inequities, we can successfully create conditions that support everyone's ability to thrive.

REFERENCES

1. Race Forward. What is racial equity? understanding key concepts related to race. Available at: https://www.raceforward.org/about/what-is-racial-equity-key-concepts. Accessed February 8, 2023.
2. Figures KD, Lhamon CE. Approaching policy with equity in mind. *Briefing Room*. March 29, 2021. Available at: https://www.whitehouse.gov/briefing-room/blog/2021/03/29/approaching-policy-with-equity-in-mind. Accessed November 18, 2022.

3. Bailey ZD, Krieger N, Agénor M, Graves J, Linos N, and Bassett MT. Structural racism and health inequities in the USA: evidence and interventions. *Lancet.* 2017;389(10077):1453–1463. Available at: https://doi.org/10.1016/S0140-6736(17)30569-X. Accessed November 18, 2022.
4. Healey R, Hinson S. The three faces of power. Grassroots Power Project. November 24, 2013. Available at: https://grassrootspowerproject.org/wp-content/uploads/2021/11/2_GPP_3FacesOfPower.pdf. Accessed November 18, 2022.
5. National Academies of Sciences, Engineering, and Medicine; Health and Medicine Division; Board on Population Health and Public Health Practice. Communities in action: pathways to health equity. National Academies Press. 2017. Available at: https://nap.nationalacademies.org/catalog/24624/communities-in-action-pathways-to-health-equity. Accessed February 2, 2023.
6. National Association for Public Health Statistics and Information Systems. USALEEP: neighborhood life expectancy project. 2021. Available at: https://www.naphsis.org/usaleep. Accessed November 18, 2022.
7. Robert Wood Johnson Foundation. Life expectancy: could where you live influence how long you live? 2020. Available at: https://www.rwjf.org/en/library/interactives/whereyouliveaffectshowlongyoulive.html. Accessed November 18, 2022.
8. Takai A, Kumar A, Kim R, Subramanian SV. Life expectancies across congressional districts in the United States. *Soc Sci Med.* 2022;298:114855. Available at: https://doi.org/10.1016/j.socscimed.2022.114855. Accessed November 18, 2022.
9. Geographic Insights Lab. Life expectancies across congressional districts in the United States. Available at: https://geographicinsights.iq.harvard.edu/CongressionalDistrict-LifeExpectancy. Accessed January 4, 2023.
10. Office of Disease Prevention and Health Promotion, US Department of Health and Human Services. Healthy People 2030: social determinants of health. Available at: https://health.gov/healthypeople/priority-areas/social-determinants-health. Accessed November 18, 2022.
11. Baltimore Development Corporation. Grocery store personal property tax credit. Available at: https://www.baltimoredevelopment.com/doing-business/grocery-store-tax-credit. Accessed February 2, 2023.
12. Dawes DE. *The Political Determinants of Health.* Baltimore, MD: Johns Hopkins University Press; 2020.
13. Givens ML, Kindig D, Inzeo PT, and Faust V. Power: the most fundamental cause of health inequity? *Health Aff.* February 1, 2018. Available at: https://www.healthaffairs.org/do/10.1377/forefront.20180129.731387. Accessed November 18, 2022.
14. Iton A, Ross RK, Tamber PS. Building community power to dismantle policy-based structural inequity in population health. *Health Aff.* 2022;41(12):1763–1771. Available at: https://doi.org/10.1377/hlthaff.2022.00540. Accessed December 31, 2022.
15. Farhang L, Morales X. Building community power to achieve health and racial equity: principles to guide transformative partnerships with local communities. National Academy of Medicine. June 13, 2022. Available at: https://doi.org/10.31478/202206d. Accessed November 18, 2022.
16. Bowleg L. "The master's tools will never dismantle the master's house": ten critical lessons for Black and other health equity researchers of color. *Health Educ Behav.* 2021;48(3):237–249. Available at: https://doi.org/10.1177/10901981211007402. Accessed February 8, 2023.

17. DeSalvo KB, Wang YC, Harris A, Auerbach J, Koo D, O'Carroll P. Public health 3.0: a call to action for public health to meet the challenges of the 21st century. *Prev Chronic Dis.* 2017;14:E78. Available at: http://dx.doi.org/10.5888/pcd14.170017. Accessed February 2, 2023.
18. Committee on Health Impact Assessment; Board on Environmental Studies and Toxicology; Division on Earth and Life Studies; National Research Council. Improving health in the United States: the role of health impact assessment. National Academies Press; 2011. Available at: https://doi.org/10.17226/13229. Accessed November 18, 2022.
19. Dannenberg AL. Effectiveness of health impact assessments: a synthesis of data from five impact evaluation reports. *Prev Chron Dis.* 2016;13:E84. Available at: https://doi.org/10.5888/pcd13.150559. Accessed December 1, 2022.
20. Sohn EK, Stein LJ, Wolpoff A, et al. Avenues of influence: the relationship between health impact assessment and determinants of health and health equity. *J Urban Health.* 2018;95(5):754–764. Available at: https://doi.org/10.1007/s11524-018-0263-5. Accessed December 31, 2022.
21. Robert Wood Johnson Foundation; PEW Charitable Trusts. HIAs and other resources to advance health-informed decisions: a toolkit to promote healthier communities through cross-sector collaboration. April 29, 2018. Available at: https://www.pewtrusts.org/en/research-and-analysis/data-visualizations/2015/hia-map?resourceTypes=Health%20notes&sortBy=relevance&sortOrder=asc&page=1. Accessed August 28, 2022.
22. Pew Charitable Trusts. Health impact project: health notes. April 7, 2021. Available at: https://www.pewtrusts.org/en/research-and-analysis/articles/2019/06/19/health-impact-project-health-notes. Accessed February 2, 2023.
23. Council Office of Racial Equity. Racial equity impact assessments. Available at: https://www.dcracialequity.org/racial-equity-impact-assessments. Accessed November 18, 2022.
24. Council Office of Racial Equity. REIA databases. Available at: https://www.dcracialequity.org/reia-database. Accessed February 2, 2023.
25. Executive Office of the President. Advancing racial equity and support for underserved communities through the federal government. *Briefing Room.* January 25, 2021. Available at: https://www.federalregister.gov/documents/2021/01/25/2021-01753/advancing-racial-equity-and-support-for-underserved-communities-through-the-federal-government. Accessed January 16, 2023.

6

Leaning In: Selecting Your Policies and Ways to Engage

You are primed and ready to engage in the policy process. You know the public health issue inside and out. Now you need to determine the best way to bring your knowledge, experience, and recommendations to the policymaking process in a way that has the greatest impact.

There are many ways to get into a swimming pool. Swan dive, cannonball, and belly flop are ways to go all in. You can carefully dip a toe or hold hands with others and walk down the steps or ladder. The same goes for getting into the policy arena. It is a reflection of personal choice, opportunity, and sometimes a decision about how much splash you want to make and how much risk you're willing to take.

This chapter focuses on the different ways that you as an individual can choose to engage in the policy process. This is not an overview of how an organization would define, develop, and launch an advocacy campaign. There are more in-depth guides for policy engagement of that scope and scale. In this chapter, we will introduce three levels of engagement that are appropriate for an individual looking to participate in building greater support for public health issues:

- Basic level: The fundamentals that every interested public health professional can and should do to help create more power for public health issues.
- Intermediate level: Focuses on specific policy issues and bringing your expertise to the policymaking process. This could include submitting comments during an agency's rulemaking process, writing a letter to the editor of your local paper, or creating a one-page memorandum to suggest policy fixes within your agency's purview.
- Advanced level: Work done in collaboration with a strategic policy campaign/initiative to facilitate change. This could include meeting with elected officials, staff, or agency representatives. It could also include acting as a resource and champion for interest groups or communities.

Examples of the types of engagement activities and general tips and tactics for effective engagement are described below.

BASIC LEVEL: HELPING BUILD POWER FOR PUBLIC HEALTH ISSUES

Congress is a stimulus response institution. And there is nothing more stimulating than having hundreds of public health professionals, families and caregivers meeting with you about an important issue.

–Edward Markey, Senator of Massachusetts[1]

Here are some fundamental steps that public health professionals can take to stimulate change and create greater support for improving health:

- Know who represents you at the local, state, and federal level. Be aware of their background and positions on policy issues related to public health and your interests.
- Track your representative's activity via their websites, subscribe to their newsletters, and follow them on social media. Engage with their content and be highly respectful in public forums. You want to be seen as a serious, solutions-oriented resource.
- Attend a town hall or other local gathering that provides an opportunity to meet your representative and forge a potential relationship. If given the opportunity to introduce yourself, be clear about who you are, what you care about, and what action you want them to take. Always be prepared with a succinct ask that resonates.
- Sign up for alerts from your professional organization. These organizations often share opportunities for engaging in targeted advocacy efforts. For example, the American Public Health Association (APHA) sends action alerts that make it quick and easy to contact your member of Congress about a specific issue or action. As Susan Polan, APHA's associate executive director, notes, "As a constituent, you are the most powerful voice for your elected representatives and a critical voice to be heard. They should never be able to say that they did not hear from the public health professionals they represent" (email, December 15, 2022).
- Register to vote if you can. Though the fight for voting rights for residing noncitizens and formerly incarcerated people continues, voting and participating in our democracy is a fundamental part of the policymaking process.

INTERMEDIATE LEVEL: BRINGING YOUR EXPERTISE TO SPECIFIC POLICY POSITIONS

Public health covers a range of issues and challenges. As you move into more in-depth levels of engagement, you can focus your efforts on specific policies rather than broad public health support. Where you start depends on where you are.

You Know Your Issue, But Not Necessarily the Specific Policy Solution

What is the big public health goal that matters to you? Are racial justice and health equity your passion? Maybe you feel strongly about environmental threats, maternal and child health, reproductive rights, substance misuse, or gun violence? Every major public health challenge we face today presents a policy opportunity. Policies and their implications are constantly being debated, legislated, and implemented at the local, state, federal, and international level. Where can you have the most impact?

First, remember that you are not alone. Policy issues are multifaceted, with many complex and nuanced factors. What might appear to be a straightforward, common-sense policy solution could have unintended consequences or impacts you aren't aware of. Passing good policies requires a village of diverse voices and constituencies, so never work alone.

Search for public health groups that align with your values and explore what policy positions they support. This includes health foundations, APHA and its state affiliates, issue-specific advocacy groups, and national agency advisory boards. These entities track policy engagement opportunities, which could illuminate a pathway for how you can be most helpful. They will most likely have done extensive policy analysis comparing different policy options, trade-offs, and impacts, and can typically provide resources on how to get involved.

Let's say, for example, you want to see more effort to address health inequities and promote policies that can improve access to healthcare. What can you do to help? One nonprofit organization—Community Catalyst—organizes advocacy coalitions to advance health policies and keeps tabs on relevant federal and state rules. On their website, they identify the short term commenting opportunities on many issues that could be informed and influenced by public health professionals. For example, Community Catalyst highlighted a proposed Center for Medicare and Medicaid Services (CMS) rule designed to reduce administrative barriers (bureaucratic rules that make it difficult to access agency services) that particularly affect people of color, older adults, people with disabilities, children, and people with high health care expenses. Community Catalyst outlined analysis and indicated how comments could be helpful for different components of the rule or for the full proposal. You can be most helpful by incorporating your data, perspectives, or experiences as they relate to the proposal.[2]

You could also play a role in local policymaking. If you happen to work inside a state agency, you could encourage the agency to submit comments to CMS. Another route is to reach out to state officials to encourage them to comment and, if rule changes are made, to encourage their efforts to implement the policy fixes.[2]

Box 6-1. Who Does an Agency Listen To?

> There are many ways to move the needle and make a difference on national environmental policy, but there is significant value in former regulators making substantive formal comments and testifying at hearings and meetings, based on decades of historical knowledge and subject matter expertise. Their understanding of the full extent of EPA's legal authority, as well as the complex political and bureaucratic structure of government, makes former regulators a sought-out and critical resource for decision-makers.

Source: Email from Betsy Southerland, former director, Office of Science & Technology, EPA Office of Water, on September 25, 2022. Reprinted with permission.

How you choose to engage is dependent on your personal interests, job restrictions, time, and opportunities. Here is a partial list of intermediate level engagement activities to consider:

- Volunteer with a policy advocacy organization by providing technical expertise or case studies to help shape their policy positions. Similarly, you can volunteer to contribute to and represent the policy positions of professional organizations. Professional organizations are numerous, ranging from nurses who work on environmental health issues to current and former governmental epidemiologists lending their expertise (see Box 6-1).
- Submit unique comments to an administrative agency that draw upon your knowledge or experience. If you are a government employee, perhaps you can catalyze your agency to submit comments. A fellow governmental entity commenting on proposed regulations can wield significant influence. The art and science of comment writing is further described in the next section.
- Seek an advisory role with local, state, or federal agencies. This could mean serving on an expert panel, reviewing their materials, and acting as a trusted, reliable resource. Advisory committees can identify policies in need of reexamination, make recommendations for fixes, and influence the process. At the federal level, there are approximately 1,000 advisory committees, which are regulated by the Federal Advisory Committee Act (FACA).[3] FACAs advise the executive branch on a wide range of health-related topics, from climate change to substance misuse.
- Consider making donations to elected officials or volunteering with campaign efforts that align with a health policy you care about. This is one route for establishing a relationship with an elected official and their team.

ADVANCED LEVEL: ACTIVE, HIGHLY PUBLIC ENGAGEMENT WITH POLICYMAKERS

Consider the important rule that the more you engage, the more you also need to know what your specific lobbying restrictions are (see Chapter 3 for details):

- Become a familiar, trusted face. In a report on how to bring greater support to the field, the Frey Evaluation LLC[4] interviewed an elected state official who had never in her 25 years in office been visited by a local public health official. You should take part in changing that dynamic, meet and get to know key policymakers, and build bridges by reaching out to officials with opposing views to find shared values and goals. Invite officials to your events to observe your operations and understand your issues. When appropriate, pepper them with positive attention in public forums, such as town halls, fundraisers, letters to the editor (LTE), and social media.
- Offer to be a resource to elected officials, their staff, and administration representatives. Translate important research for them. Help draft legislative language, rules language, and oversight letters. Design questions for testimony participants from different constituencies. For example, if you have a relationship with a policymaker and know that hearings will be held on your issue, you can draft key questions for them to ask your opposition. You may have far more insight into opposition arguments and the playbook they are using to stymy good policy. You can help prepare for hearings by suggesting who should testify, prepare witnesses, and develop talking points for the policymaking team. The earlier you are engaged in the process, the more impact you can have on policy outcomes.
- Lend your credibility and be a public voice. Engage in writing op-eds and LTEs or testify in public hearings. Policymakers read newspapers and high-profile media sources as a way to stay up to date on emerging issues that their constituents care about. They or their staff will routinely read local letters to the editors, editorial board opinions, and op-eds. Using any of these vehicles is a great way to get exposure and reach large audiences at no cost.
- Whether you work at a government agency or in a business that impacts public health, you should try to influence policy positions within your organization.

While we have focused on public policies, policymaking is not limited to the government. The business sector can have enormous influence on policymakers. Businesses can also determine their own policies and practices that significantly affect health, such as policies related to sick-leave benefits or vaccination requirements. For example, a city government might not have authority to require businesses to have paid sick-leave policies, but you could work with companies to establish pro-health policies and positions. You should think broadly about opportunities to engage with the private sector as allies.

DRILLING DOWN INTO SKILLS AND APPROACHES

Every public health professional can choose engagement approaches that appeal to their individual interests and abilities. For instance, writing an effective op-ed requires strong writing skills, knowledge of how to frame a message, and an understanding of how to engage your target audience with a compelling hook. Meeting directly with an elected official or testifying before a regulatory agency taps into different skills and abilities. This section provides how-tos for a variety of effective engagements with policymakers.

Interacting With Policymakers

Whether you have a one-on-one meeting with a policymaker or are engaging in larger forums, there are a few fundamental considerations. Ask staffers about the best way to be helpful and heard. Do not be offended if the elected official does not show up and sends their staff instead. Staffers are often the engine behind positions, statements, and critical policy work, so don't underestimate how productive and impactful these engagements can be.

- Always have an ask. This cannot be overemphasized. What specific recommendation or action do you want the policymaker to take? Seize that moment, tell them (nicely) what they need to do and why. Too often, presenters squander this opportunity and do not provide a specific, measurable ask. How can you hold a decision-maker accountable if you have not given them a definable action?
- Be concise and factual, but don't bury your message. When giving testimony and answering follow-up questions, it is essential to be succinct. You have limited time and attention, so be sure policymakers hear and remember your primary message and request. If you give long winded answers or lengthy sentences, you will lose their engagement. Also, avoid using technical jargon. Policymakers are rarely experts in public health. By using insider or academic language, you risk alienating your audience or causing your point to be misunderstood. Translate your words and phrases the way you would with the general public. Ask yourself, would my grandmother understand what I just said (assuming she isn't a public health professional)?
- Be prepared to counter your opposition. Know the points being made by those opposed to the policy. In public health, opposition often centers on concerns about economic loss, personal freedoms, or misinformation. Be primed to address their concerns head on with succinct counter-information, framed in a way that will resonate with the critic. You can either be proactive and incorporate these issues into your remarks and formal materials, or you can have a prepared response ready if questions arise (see Box 6-2).
- Be polite and positive. No matter what, you should project confidence with a sense of polite deference to the policymakers. Under no circumstances should you take comments or questions personally. Even if questions seem uncharitable or contentious, do not become defensive or reactive. It can be easy to misinterpret the intent of a question in these high-pressure situations. It is also possible that the question or comment was meant to evoke a negative response as a means of undermining your position. Do not

Box 6-2. Ready, Set, SNAP

During a visit to a conservative Congressman's office about expanding the Supplemental Nutrition Assistance Program (SNAP), a staffer railed against "lazy people who want handouts and don't want to work." Being prepared, we had data showing the percent of people who work that receive SNAP. Then we brought out data we knew would resonate. This member was a strong advocate of children's health, so we made the point very clearly (reinforced with our one-page leave behind) that if a household receives SNAP benefits, all children in the household who attend school automatically qualify for free school meals, an important step toward alleviating child hunger. The look on this staffer's face was priceless! He assured us he would highlight this connection between SNAP, school meals, and children's health with their member.

-Keshia Pollack Porter, PhD, MPH

take the bait. Neutralize their negativity and remain polite and positive. Thank the policymaker before and after each interaction.

- Passion. We all care immensely about the work we do. Many times, we bring personal stories and truths to our efforts. Often, our positions reflect profound moral values. That said, you must respect that opposing positions may be founded on equally strong beliefs, which may be different from yours. It is fine to show you care and to bring heart to your cause, but be careful not to imply that a decision-maker is immoral or amoral if they do not follow your recommendations. It is difficult to get people to agree with you if they feel attacked or defensive.
- Beware of humor. Many of us use humor to help diffuse tense situations, manage conflict, or to create comfort and connection. Resist. Resist. Resist. You can only engage with humor if you are one hundred percent certain that your audience will understand and appreciate it. Just like text messages or emails, a comment meant to be humorous can easily be misinterpreted. Five policymakers may find it funny, but one may be put off. Was it worth it? In general, despite the fact that we can all use a good laugh, humor is not worth the risk in this setting.
- Avoid being cynical or sarcastic. Your job is to be seen as solution-oriented. Cynicism, which comes from a belief that self-interest is the ultimate motive behind all human actions,[5] counteracts that image. Avoid coming across as snide and mocking. You are there for a common good. A dark view will cast a shadow on your recommendation and may divert attention away from your intention.

Testifying Before Policymakers

Testifying happens in all three branches of government (legislative, executive, and judicial). Legislative hearings are an important part of the decision-making process. They can contribute to an investigation, inform potential legislation or appropriations budgets, and help vet a political nominee. Testimony can also be provided in hearings for public commenting or fact gathering with agencies. In Congress, testimony is given daily across the many committees. This is also true at the state, county, city, and local levels. Testifying before a court of law is a different skill and competency, which we will not cover here. Research on how testimony influences state legislators shows that lawmakers, regardless of party affiliation, found testimony influential, especially when presented by credible, knowledgeable, and unbiased individuals.[6] While testimony generally does not make or break a policy, important opportunities can arise from engaging with policymakers and their staff in this way.

- Testimony is an opportunity to frame the issue using a public health perspective in a way that focuses on why the issue matters and emphasize what needs to be done.
- Your testimony may be the first time a legislator has focused on or learned details about your issue. Staff are often the ones focusing on the details, so treat this as an opportunity to educate policymakers. Providing testimony is a chance for you to catalyze legislators and their staff to further research the issue and consider your position.
- Giving testimony is an opportunity for you to shine as an expert and to develop relationships with policymakers, their staff, and potential media, which can position you as a resource for the future.

Providing testimony or comments is a key opportunity for bringing attention to your policy position. How you package your information and present it is critical for success.

Oral and Written Testimony Are Different

Each policy venue has its own rules and guidance for how testimony is to be provided. In many instances, there is an opportunity to submit written testimony, even if it won't be presented orally.

Oral testimony differs from written testimony in a number of ways. Typically for oral testimony, a short period of time is allotted, two to ten minutes, rarely more (closer to two minutes is the norm). When preparing oral testimony, optimize your testimony for listeners, not readers. Design your testimony to reflect how you speak so that it comes across as natural and not stilted. Do not use words that cause you to stumble or grammar that feels awkward to you. Craft your testimony so that the listener will find it compelling and engaging.

Written testimony can contain far more detail than oral testimony. In most instances, written testimony can be longer as well. In general, written testimony is for the staff behind the scenes and is an opportunity to provide more detail, facts, and figures. That said, it is still important to translate data and limit jargon. In the Appendices at the end of this book, we provide resources on how to best structure written testimony.

Prepare an Abbreviated Testimony

Inevitably, at some point you will find yourself in a situation where your testimony gets cut short unexpectedly. Suddenly, a vote is called and members need to leave. Maybe someone before you spoke too long. Similar to how you would use an elevator speech, be prepared to boil it down to your key messages and ask. What do you want them to remember?

Engaging in Agency Rulemaking Processes

Another way to influence the policymaking process is through participating in public comment periods during the rulemaking process. Typically, rulemaking is initiated by a legal mandate where Congress, or the authorizing legislative body, gives the agency authority to determine how to implement a law. But rulemaking can also be initiated within an agency when there are administrative challenges, lack of clarity, or other logistical problems, such as viability of enforcing rules. Professionals within an agency can help identify issues and solutions. In addition, outside individuals or organizations can petition the agency to modify or change its rules. For instance, a coalition of environmental, health, and consumer groups have petitioned FDA to ban the dangerous class of chemicals from all use in foods and food packaging.[7] Lastly, public health professionals serving on federal advisory committees can also make recommendations to agencies regarding rules.

Public comments can make a big difference, especially at the federal level where there are strict processes in place to ensure the public has the opportunity to provide input on proposed rules and regulations. Key stakeholders, such as Congress, the executive branch, academics, and the general public, can influence the rulemaking process. Engaging in the agency rulemaking process can have a very real impact and is an important opportunity in which facts matter. Government regulators routinely note that generic statements of support or opposition and form letters consisting of boilerplate language sent multiple times have little to no influence on a rulemaking process. Regulators' decisions are informed by sound reasoning, not by a majority vote. Ten thousand form letters carry less weight than one concise, evidence-based public comment that addresses the specific issue the agency is tackling. When submitting comments, take the opportunity to present your knowledge, experience, and research in a succinct and impactful way.

Here are the basics:

- Focus on the sections of the rule on which you can offer direct evidence or perspective. You do not have to comment on the entire proposal. The more detailed and constructive your insights are, the better.

- Identify the specific issue you will address in your comments. Rules may have many different elements, and the agency could be dealing with thousands of comments. Identify the topic using a header. If relevant, identify the page, paragraph, and any other identifiers from the original governmental notice.
- Provide relevant evidence and citations to support your positions. Go in with the mindset that you are providing technical support to the agency so that the rule in question can withstand potential review in a court of administrative law (or if you're opposed, present data that could be used in a law case brought against the rule).
- If you disagree with the proposed action, you are more likely to influence the agency if you explain with present evidence as to why their regulation is harmful and provide an alternative solution. Explain why your alternative is practical, potentially more effective, and better for meeting the agency's objective.
- Be sure to include a short paragraph of credentials that illustrates why they should consider your facts and heed your recommendations.
- Explain the pros, cons, and trade-offs of your position, especially if you can address them with solid evidence and good reasoning.
- If you have questions or do not understand the agency's request for information, you can reach out to the agency's designated contact person. Be polite to this person and listen carefully.

It is particularly helpful if you understand the regulatory challenge and can provide explicit research, experience, or knowledge that directly answers the agency's question (see Box 6-3). Put yourself in their shoes and help guide them toward positive public health outcomes.

Using the Media to Indirectly Inform Policymakers

Policymakers pay attention to what the media covers and what their constituents are reading. It's one key way to get a handle on their jurisdiction's mood or what hot topics they should prioritize and address in their work. There are many ways for you to engage with the media as a vehicle for getting your policy on their radar.

Box 6-3. Quality Versus Quantity

> Agencies need to show that there is evidence to support its decisions. Your well-written, data-based submission can be the evidence an agency needs to support an important policy. As a regulator, I found that the number of comments received does not matter-the regulatory process is not a popularity contest. What is important is the applicability of the information you submit to the problem the agency is trying to solve.

Source: Email from Dr. David Michaels, professor at George Washington University Milken Institute and former Occupational Safety and Health Administration administrator, October 10, 2022. Reprinted with permission.

In general, a succinct LTE (typically 250–500 words) is the easiest to get placed with a media outlet, while op-eds (generally 600–700 words) tend to be more difficult because of the high volume of submissions and competing interests. Trying to get placement in major daily papers, like the *New York Times* or *Washington Post*, is a lofty goal for advancing national policy. It is more realistic, and often just as powerful, to focus on local media outlets. Policymakers can be especially sensitive to hometown coverage. Many local papers, particularly those with limited numbers of reporters covering health beats, may be hungry for thoughtful content from experts like yourself. As a retired commentary page editor of the Philadelphia Inquirer noted, "We have problems sometimes in getting op-eds on local and regional issues."[8(p8)]

Writing an op-ed is an art. It is not simply a recitation of facts but rather a well-written piece that presents a unique perspective and solution and that hooks the reader. Here are the basic rules of thumb:

- Start with a hook. Open with an attention-grabbing fact or a concise, compelling story. You want to draw the reader in so that they finish the entire piece.
- Explain the context and why the issue matters. Lay out compelling evidence that best highlights the issue and the solution.
- Write for your audience. Avoid technical, academic phrases and public health jargon. Be succinct and avoid cliches, sarcasm, and unnecessarily partisan language (see Box 6-4).[9]
- End with a concrete, tangible call to action. What can the reader reasonably do to help? The more specific, the better.

Direct Meetings With Policymakers

Meetings are more likely to happen when there is an existing relationship, either through your affiliated organizations or your own individual relationships. When seeking meetings with elected officials, the door opens more easily if you are a constituent (don't be surprised if, when you go on the visit, you are asked, where do you live?), a donor/volunteer, or they are already familiar with you because of your media work or involvement in past events.[10]

Box 6-4. Write to Be Heard

> Are you speaking to scientists or to the public, press, and policymakers? Use language that resonates and makes sense to your audience. Notice the difference in how the same information is presented:
>
> - Technical: "We conducted a longitudinal analysis of 900 men and found that the odds of myocardial infarction (MI) were 3.45 times greater in smokers than in nonsmokers."
> - Real world lay: "Men who smoke are more than three times more likely to have a heart attack than men who don't."[9]

Meeting with staff, rather than the lead official, is normal at the federal, state, and, to a lesser degree, the local level unless you have a long-standing relationship with the official. Treat staff with the same regard you would treat the official themself. The staff are the ones getting things done behind the scene, including drafting legislation, rules, regulations, budgets, and other policy related matters.

It is a good idea to write a one-page summary of your issue and include your contact information to leave behind. The staff that you met with will likely refer to it when updating their official on meetings they had. The one-page document should embrace the rules mentioned above and be visually appealing. Although we are referring to it as a one-pager, printing double-sided allows for space to add important references and citations in support of the points you shared during the meeting. Finally, it is good practice to send a thank you message to the staff and/or official after your meeting and to follow up when there are updates on the policy.

Key Takeaways

- There are many ways and different levels (basic, intermediate, advanced) to engage in the policy process. Choose ones that appeal to your individual interests and abilities.
- Don't underestimate the value and impact of meeting with legislative and regulatory staffers. Staffers are often the engines behind positions, statements, and critical policy work.
- Provide testimony or written comments as a key opportunity to bring attention to your policy positions. How you package and present your position is critical for success.
- Participate in the government agency rulemaking process by submitting public comments on proposed rules.
- Use media advocacy, such as letters to the editor and op-eds, to indirectly inform policymakers.

REFERENCES

1. American Public Health Association. The power of advocacy. Available at: https://www.apha.org/-/media/files/pdf/advocacy/power_of_advocacy.ashx. Accessed November 18, 2022.
2. Reusch C. Proposed CMS rule would reduce administrative barriers that keep people from enrolling in and keeping their health coverage. Community Catalyst. October 12, 2022. Available at: https://communitycatalyst.org/posts/proposed-cms-rule-would-reduce-administrative-barriers-that-keep-people-from-enrolling-in-and-keeping-their-health-coverage. Accessed February 2, 2023.
3. US General Services Administration. The Federal Advisory Committee Act (FACA) brochure. Available at: https://www.gsa.gov/policy-regulations/policy/federal-advisory-committee-management/advice-and-guidance/the-federal-advisory-committee-act-faca-brochure. Accessed November 18, 2022.
4. Frey Evaluation LLC. Fighting for public health: findings, opportunities, and next steps from a feasibility study to strengthen public health advocacy. Network for Public Health Law. September 2022. Available at: https://www.networkforphl.org/wp-content/uploads/2022/09/Fight-for-Public-Health-Findings-Opportunities-and-Next-Steps-from-a-Feasibility-Study-to-Strengthen-Public-Health-Advocacy.pdf. Accessed November 18, 2022.

5. Stavrova O, Ehlebracht D. The cynical genius illusion: exploring and debunking lay beliefs about cynicism and competence. *Pers Soc Psychol Rev*. 2019;45(2):254–269. Available at: https://doi.org/10.1177/0146167218783195. Accessed December 1, 2022.
6. Moreland-Russell S, Barbero C, Andersen S, Geary N, Dodson EA, Brownson RC. "Hearing from all sides" how legislative testimony influences state level policymakers in the United States. *Int J Health Policy Manag*. 2015;4(2):91–98. Available at: https://www.ijhpm.com/article_2941_5c372898132edf73c4f2d46ca265ba16.pdf. Accessed December 1, 2022.
7. Environmental Defense Fund, Breast Cancer Prevention Partners, Center for Environmental Health, et al. Citizens petition requesting that the agency take more aggressive action to protect consumers from per- and poly-fluroalkyl substances (PFAS) by banning all forms that biopersist in the human body. June 3, 2021. Available at: https://blogs.edf.org/health/files/2021/06/PFAS-Petition-to-FDA-FINAL-6-1-21.pdf. Accessed November 18, 2022.
8. Zeck D, Rennolds E. *Op-Eds: A Cost-Effective Strategy for Advocacy*. Evanston, IL: Benton Foundation; 1990. Available at: https://namp.americansforthearts.org/by-program/reports-and-data/legislation-policy/naappd/op-eds-a-cost-effective-strategy-for-advocacy. Accessed November 18, 2022.
9. Cobb L, Driver CR, Tabac L. Communicating with data: a guide to writing public health data reports. Vital Strategies, Bloomberg Philanthropies. May 14, 2018. Available at: https://www.vitalstrategies.org/wp-content/uploads/PHP_WritingGuide_v07.pdf. Accessed December 31, 2022.
10. Advocacy and Communication Solutions. Five rules for policymaker engagement. 2015. Available at: https://www.advocacyandcommunication.org/wp-content/themes/acs/docs/resources/policy_maker_engagement_December_2015/ACS_Five_Rules_Poliymaker_Engagement-1-1.pdf. Accessed November 18, 2022.

7

Ready, Set, But Don't Go Alone

If you want to go fast, go alone. If you want to go far, go together.
—African proverb

Today's public health challenges are complex and involve multiple constituencies, jurisdictions, and interests. Whether you want to work at the national, state, tribal, or local level, each has unique dynamics and factors that influence which policies are viable and which are dead ends. The process can be daunting and fraught to navigate alone. Successful policy engagement requires a team effort. A single voice can get lost or drowned out in our bustling world. Whether you are protesting in the street or proposing to revamp an agency's rule, it is more effective and strategic to do so with a village. The good news is, in most situations, there are organizations, health associations, and communities that have long been engaged with your topic and understand the local context. You should determine which village is right for you and your issue area.

THE POLICY VILLAGE

For any policy issue, there are likely those who benefit and those who have something to lose. Public health, as a field, is typically invested in the common good, which may be in direct conflict with capitalist motivations or the religious, cultural, or personal values of some. Political scientists roughly categorize the most common interest groups as business and industry, professional associations, labor groups, public interest organizations, and governmental officials.[1(p47)] These interest groups can have considerable influence on policymakers by blocking proposed policies or proposing alternative policies that may serve to advance their interests.

Many organizations have publicly stated visions for change and policy action plans for short-, intermediate-, and long-term policy goals. Think broadly. There is a wide range of groups engaged in the policymaking process, from governmental institutions (e.g., CDC), to philanthropies (e.g., the Robert Wood Johnson Foundation, de Beaumont Foundation), and nonprofits focused in specific areas (e.g., the Sierra Club, the American Heart Association). There are also many relevant local groups, some working as chapters affiliated with national groups and others that are more community-based.

These players have a pulse on which policymakers are supportive or opposed, what obstacles need to be overcome, and how you can help.

Assess who aligns most with your interests and values by asking yourself some questions. Is there a state association that could help with content? Are there local groups who might be interested, such as religious organizations, PTAs, community groups, or local foundations? Who can give greater perspective on how the issue fits into the larger context of challenges and issues? Who is opposed? Are there competing interests? Does the community care but have higher priorities they want addressed? Do you need to work on other priorities first to help set the stage and develop strong relationships? Listening and aligning with community interests is key for short- and long-term effectiveness.

Appendix A contains a list of organizations that provide roadmaps on public health policies, opportunities for engagement, and starting points for determining what policies are ripe for opportunity.

A LOOK AT THE PUBLIC HEALTH POLICY LANDSCAPE: WHERE ARE YOU NEEDED?

Public policy has always been a core lever for improving public health. The greatest health achievements of the twentieth century, and the primary reason we live longer today, occurred through public policy wins. But recently, the United States has been faltering. While the COVID-19 pandemic shortened life expectancy in all countries, the United States is the only developed country in which the downward trend continued. This is in part due to widening health disparities, opioid and violence crises, and a generally under-supported public health and healthcare system.[2] Now, more than ever, we need to strengthen and utilize the public policy levers.

One direction is to focus on assuring that high-impact policies in some parts of the country get put into place for everyone, regardless of where people live, work, pray, or play. CDC's HI-5 initiative, the CityHealth policy package, and the County Health Rankings are just a handful of lists of opportunities.[3-5] Another area for engagement is halting the attacks against public health agency authorities, funding, and programs. The third area of opportunity is advancing the next generation of policies that can enhance our health (see Table 7-1).

WHAT WILL IT TAKE IN THESE CHALLENGING TIMES?

Working to advance public health has always been challenging. It can require decades of persistent, incremental work. Sometimes there are setbacks and progress is rolled back. This is a reality that almost every health issue faces at one time or another. Competing priorities, viewpoints, and interests are the norm, even within your own village.

Table 7-1. Examples of Future Potential Health Wins and Associated Policies

Policy Area	Evidence-based Policy Examples
Infectious disease control	Minimum funding requirements for health department capacity; strengthen agency authorities
Motor vehicle safety	Complete street policies and Safe System, climate related policies on electrification, vision zero policies, 0.04 blood alcohol concentration limit laws to reduce drunk driving
Safer and healthier foods	Unified food safety agency, sugar-sweetened beverage restrictions, school meal programs, restrict toxic food additives, Food Safety and Modernization Act, environmentally-preferred purchasing policies, healthy food purchasing policies
Safer workplaces	Paid sick leave, comprehensive workplace safety programs, mental health and wellness policies, repeal "bring your gun to work" laws
Tobacco control	Restrictions on e-cigarettes, flavor restrictions, smoke-free indoor air policies
Family planning	Expanding pool of clinicians offering abortion services (RNs, midwives, physician assistants, etc.), expanding access to doula care, paid family leave
Gun violence prevention	Domestic violence and extreme risk protection orders, firearm purchaser licensing, limit concealed and open carry laws, repeal "Stand Your Ground" laws, safe storage (i.e., child access prevention)

Many people in the United States, especially from historically marginalized and oppressed communities, have been failed by public policy and entire systems.[2] Unequivocally, we must all work to dismantle and obliterate structural racism in all forms, especially those that harm health and contribute to inequities. It took hundreds of years to build this country, so we won't be able to tear down racist and unjust systems overnight, but we can utilize policy change to right the wrongs and create a more equitable society where everyone can thrive.

Persistence Pays

All policy development, passage, and implementation takes time. The rule of thumb is a minimum three to five years, sometimes longer, to go from policy development to getting a law on the books (we acknowledge that local level policy change may take considerably less time). There are always roadblocks and rollercoasters. The most common advice from high-impact advocates is to be persistent. Don't give up when the odds seem stacked against you.

A few simple ways to stay the course are listed as follows:

- Always remember why you care about the issue. Keep your big picture goal in mind.
- Focus on strategic objectives that can help better position the policy, such as building support, allyships, and greater societal understanding for the issue.
- Avoid burnout by working with people you enjoy. Take time to care for your own physical and mental health.
- Celebrate the small wins. Make your allies and political champions feel appreciated.

Be Open and Willing to Forge Unusual Alliances

To move a policy, there can be strength in the number of supporters, but there can also be great power in demonstrating a broad spectrum of support. Bipartisan support always improves the chances of a policy win. Policy solutions can gain momentum and policymaker interest when many different constituencies join forces. Having the local hospital, Chamber of Commerce, Parent Teachers Association, or local union speak in unity can be a game changer. Never assume that an organization that fought against one public health policy in the past will fight against all future policies.

Civic engagement relies on civil relationships. Are there interest organizations that might share common values on an issue or entities within an organization that might splinter off from their pack to support a policy? Perhaps you or a colleague work in a business, agency, or organization that could benefit from uncharacteristically engaging in a public health policy debate (think of this as a great opportuntity for you to make an insider's case for engagement). Potential champions can emerge from unexpected places when we are open to finding shared values and interests.

Your Credibility Is Your Greatest Asset

As a public health professional, you are a tremendous asset in the policymaking process. You offer policymakers, interest groups, and communities a vital source of scientific knowledge, experience, and expertise. Your involvement can have a significant impact, which is why you must focus on evidence, avoid hyperbole, and be your authentic self. Make sure your stories are genuine and real. Be a thoughtful, honest broker of information. Trust is not a renewable resource.

FINAL THOUGHTS

This book is designed to inspire public health professionals and introduce you to the basics of policymaker engagement. It is an introductory field guide for public health professionals rather than a detailed how-to manual for more advanced policy work, such as creating issue campaigns, conducting media advocacy, organizing grassroots or grass top constituencies, and other comprehensive policy advocacy initiatives. In Appendix B, we provide resources to help you explore these and other policy engagement skills in more depth.

For those of you at the beginning of your journey to become a more effective advocate, we thank you for taking the first step by reading this book. We encourage you to keep building your policy engagement muscles by participating in trainings, workshops, and seizing opportunities to develop your skills. We hope that one day every single public health professional will not only understand the role policy plays in advancing public health, but also know how to effectively engage in policymaking for real-world change. You are a part of that change. With your work and engagement, it is possible, not just aspirational, to create a healthier nation for all.

Key Takeaways
- Your participation in the policymaking process is critical, but you don't need to do it alone. There is a large ecosystem of organizations and communities for you to tap into and coordinate with.
- There is still a lot to be done to advance the public's health and a whole next generation of policies waiting to be moved and advanced with your help.
- Always be persistent, guard your credibility, and be willing to listen and collaborate with unlikely allies.

REFERENCES

1. Kingdon JW. *Agendas, Alternatives, and Public Policies: Updated Edition with an Epilogue on Health Care.* 2nd ed. London, UK: Pearson; 2011.
2. Bloomberg American Health Initiative. Reversing the decline: 10 ideas to improve life expectancy. Johns Hopkins Bloomberg School of Public Health. Available at: https://americanhealth.jhu.edu/sites/default/files/website-media/resources/LifeExpec_Report.pdf. Accessed February 21, 2023.
3. Centers for Disease Control and Prevention. The HI-5 interventions. Last reviewed June 28, 2021. Available at: https://www.cdc.gov/policy/opaph/hi5/interventions/index.html. Accessed February 21, 2023.
4. de Beaumont Foundation, Kaiser Permanente. Our policy package. CityHealth. Available at: https://www.cityhealth.org/our-policy-package. Accessed February 21, 2023.
5. County Health Rankings. County health rankings & roadmaps. 2023. Available at: https://www.countyhealthrankings.org. Accessed February 21, 2023.

Appendix A: Organizations

This appendix is a brief list of organizations that provide roadmaps on public health policies, opportunities for engagement, and starting points for determining what policies are ripe for you.

American Public Health Association (APHA): In coordination with its members and state and regional affiliates, APHA works with key decision-makers to shape public policy to address today's ongoing public health concerns. For further information, visit: https://www.apha.org/Policies-and-Advocacy/Advocacy-for-Public-Health.

State and Regional Public Health Associations: Champion the same goals as APHA to promote, protect, and advocate for the public's health. They are independently established and have their own infrastructure, policies, processes, and procedures. APHA affiliates participate, implement, and advocate on behalf of various public health issues. For further information, visit: https://www.apha.org/APHA-Communities/Affiliates/State-and-Regional-Public-Health-Associations.

Association of State and Territorial Health Officials: Offers policy and advocacy resources to shape laws, regulations, and administrative actions that drive improvement in governmental public health agencies. For further information, visit: https://www.astho.org/advocacy/.

Big Cities Health Coalition: A forum for America's largest metropolitan health departments, leveraging the power of a collective voice to impact policies and decision-making in the federal government. For further information, visit: https://www.bigcitieshealth.org/advocacy/.

Campaign for Tobacco Free Kids: Provides tools designed to help public health advocates conduct effective campaigns to enact and implement laws that save lives. For further information, visit: https://www.tobaccofreekids.org/advocacy-tools.

Change Lab Solutions: A nonpartisan nonprofit organization that uses the tools of law and policy to advance health equity. They partner with communities across the nation to improve health and opportunity by changing harmful laws, policies, and systems. For further information, visit: https://www.changelabsolutions.org/.

CityHealth: An initiative of de Beaumont Foundation and Kaiser Permanente. They rate 75 of the nation's largest cities on policies that can make real, lasting impacts in people's everyday quality of life. They offer reports, news, and tools to expand access for all city residents to live in a safe and thriving environment and have a healthy body and mind. For further information, visit: https://www.cityhealth.org/resource-center/?resource_category=tool.

Community Catalyst: Partners with local, state, and national organizations and leaders to leverage and build power so that people are at the center of important decisions about health and health care. Their work focuses on rigorous policy analysis and research, multi-state advocacy campaigns, strategic communications, organizing, and coalition building. For further information, visit: https://communitycatalyst.org.

Community Toolbox: A service of the Center for Community Health and Development at the University of Kansas that offers help assessing community needs and resources, addressing social determinants of health, engaging stakeholders, action planning, building leadership, improving cultural competency, planning an evaluation, and sustaining your efforts over time. Their Advocating for Change toolkit supports planning for advocacy efforts and responding to opposition. For further information, visit: https://ctb.ku.edu/en/advocating-change.

Inseparable: A coalition of people from across the country who share a common goal to fundamentally improve mental health care policy. For further information, visit: https://www.inseparable.us/.

Lerner Center for Public Health Advocacy: Trains leaders as effective advocates for solving the world's greatest public health challenges and offers resources to ensure that future public health leaders are fluent in advocacy, including sophisticated communications, social marketing, and health promotion and policy engagement skills. For further information, visit: https://www.jhsph.edu/research/centers-and-institutes/lerner-center-for-public-health-advocacy/.

National Association of City and County Health Officials: Serves as the national voice for local health departments and plays a critical role in Washington, DC advocating for local public health with federal policymakers. Their Advocacy Toolkit provides a starting point to help you understand the ins and outs of communicating with members of Congress. For further information, visit: https://www.naccho.org/uploads/downloadable-resources/Advocacy-Toolkit-February-2023.pdf.

Network for Public Health Law: Provides nonpartisan legal technical assistance and resources, collaborating with a broad set of partners across sectors to expand and enhance the use of practical legal and policy solutions. They offer biweekly e-newsletters (*Network Report* and *Judicial Trends*) for insights and commentary on law and policy in public health. For further information, visit: https://www.networkforphl.org.

Robert Wood Johnson Foundation: The largest US philanthropy devoted to health maintains a collection of policy-related briefs that explain many policy issues in a concise, easily digestible format. They also have a Communications Toolbox that will show you how to find important audiences, translate your work, and compel action so many others can benefit. For further information, visit: https://www.rwjf.org/en/insights/advocacy-and-policy.html?o=2&us=1 and https://www.rwjf.org/communicationstoolbox/communications-resources.html.

Trust for America's Health: A nonpartisan public health policy, research and advocacy organization that prioritizes prevention and health equity as foundational to policymaking. They develop reports, other resources, and initiatives, and recommend policies. For further information, visit: https://www.tfah.org/issues.

County Health Rankings and Roadmaps: A program of the University of Wisconsin Population Health Institute, which provides data, evidence, guidance, and examples to build awareness of the multiple factors that influence health and support leaders in growing community power to improve health equity. Their Action Center offers action learning guides on many topics. For further information, visit: https://www.countyhealthrankings.org/take-action-to-improve-health/action-center.

Appendix B: Advocacy and Policy Change Resources

This appendix is a brief list of key resources that will allow you to explore in more depth topic areas covered in the book.

COALITIONS AND PARTNERSHIPS

- Creating and Maintaining Coalitions and Partnerships: https://ctb.ku.edu/en/creating-and-maintaining-coalitions-and-partnerships

FEDERAL BUDGET PROCESS

- The Federal Budget Process 101 by Alessandra Zimmermann: https://www.aaas.org/news/federal-budget-process-101

GRASSROOTS ORGANIZING

- Midwest Academy: http://www.midwestacademy.com/
- Health In All Policies Resources: https://www.cdc.gov/policy/hiap/index.html

LEGISLATIVE HEALTH NOTES

- Johns Hopkins Bloomberg School of Public Health: Health In All Policies Research Center: https://publichealth.jhu.edu/institute-for-health-and-social-policy/our-work/health-in-all-policies-research-center

LOBBYING

- Complying with Anti-Lobbying Rules: https://www.changelabsolutions.org/product/complying-anti-lobbying-rules

MEDIA ADVOCACY

- Media Advocacy: Lessons From Community Experiences by DH Jernigan and PA Wright: https://pubmed.ncbi.nlm.nih.gov/8918021

PUBLIC HEALTH ADVOCACY OVERVIEW

- *Advocacy for Public Health Policy Change: An Urgent Imperative* by Harry M. Snyder, JD, and Anthony B. Iton, MD, JD, MPH: https://ajph.aphapublications.org/doi/book/10.2105/9780875533148
- The Lerner Center for Public Health Advocacy: Resources: https://publichealth.jhu.edu/lerner-center/resources

WRITING OP-EDS

- The OpEd Project: https://www.theopedproject.org

Appendix C: Abbreviations

ACA: Affordable Care Act
ACF: Administration for Children and Families
ACL: Administration for Community Living
AHRQ: Agency for Healthcare Research and Quality
APHA: American Public Health Association
ATSDR: Agency for Toxic Substances and Disease Registry
ASTHO: Association of State and Territorial Health Officials
BRFSS: Behavioral Risk Factor Surveillance System
CEO: chief executive officer
CEPH: Council for Education of Public Health
CDC: Centers for Disease Control and Prevention
CMS: Center for Medicare and Medicaid Services
CORE: Council Office of Racial Equity (Washington, DC)
COVID-19: coronavirus disease 2019
EPA: US Environmental Protection Agency
FACA: Federal Advisory Committee Act
FDA: US Food and Drug Administration
HCPH: Harris County Public Health (Texas)
HHS: US Department of Health and Human Services
HIA: Health Impact Assessment
HI-5: Health Impact in 5 Years
HRSA: Health Resources and Services Administration
IHS: Indian Health Service
LTE: letters to the editor
MI: myocardial infarction
NACCHO: National Association of County and City Health Officials
NAS: National Academies of Science
NIH: National Institutes of Health
NGO: nongovernmental organization
OMB: Office of Management and Budget
OSHA: Occupational Safety and Health Administration
PFAS: polyfluoroalkyl substances

PRAMS: Pregnancy Risk Assessment Monitoring System
REIA: Racial Equity Impact Assessment
ROPS: rollover protective structures
RWJF: Robert Wood Johnson Foundation
SAMHSA: Substance Abuse and Mental Health Services Administration
SDOH: social determinants of health
SNAP: Supplemental Nutrition Assistance Program
T21: Tobacco 21
USDA: US Department of Agriculture

About the Authors

Shelley Hearne, DrPH, MPH, is the Deans Sommer & Klag Professor for Public Health Advocacy and director, Lerner Center for Public Health Advocacy at the Johns Hopkins Bloomberg School of Public Health. She brings over three decades of policymaking experience in government, nonprofits, and philanthropy, including founder and inaugural executive director of Trust for America's Health. She has routinely worked with legislators, executives, and regulators at the city, state, and federal level to advance environmental, health, and financial security wins for the public.

Keshia M. Pollack Porter, PhD, MPH, is a Bloomberg Centennial Professor and the Bloomberg Centennial Chair of the Department of Health Policy and Management at the Johns Hopkins Bloomberg School of Public Health. She is a health equity scholar whose research advances policies that create safe and healthy environments where people live, work, play, and travel, with an emphasis on addressing structural drivers of health and promoting effective cross-sector collaborations. She has over 15 years of directly engaging with policymakers to achieve health equity using tools such as health impact assessment and legislative health notes.

Katrina S. Forrest, JD, is the Co-Executive Director of City Health, where she collaborates closely with municipal leaders, policy experts, and other stakeholders to expand the understanding of health beyond healthcare and drive municipal policy change to improve the conditions that most influence a person's health. She brings over a decade of policymaking experience in nonprofits and state and local government, having previously worked for elected leaders in Washington, DC, the city of Chicago, and for the state of Illinois on issues of health, transportation, housing, and economic justice.

Index

Note: Italicized page references indicate Figures, Tables, or Illustrations.

A

abbreviated testimony, preparation of, 75
Activist Lab, of Boston University, 4
adjudication, of health, 26, *27,* 28
Administration for Children and Families (ACF), 33
Administration for Community Living (ACL), 34
administrative agency, submitting of comments to, 70
advanced level, of policymaking engagement, 67, 78
advisory role, with agency, 70
advocacy
    American Public Health Association on, 1–2, 5
    mental health care policy and, 24
    policy organizations for, 2, 70
Advocacy for Public Health Policy Change (Snyder and Iton), 91
Affordable Care Act (ACA), 18
agencies
    advisory role with, 70
    collaborations with nonprofits of, 69–70, 81–82
    federal health, 23–24
    human service, 33–34
    public health and, 23, 70
    rulemaking process of, 24–25, 75
Agency for Healthcare Research and Quality (AHRQ), 32
Agency for Toxic Substances and Disease Registry (ATSDR), 32
agency rulemaking process, 24–25
    public comments in, 75–77, 78
airbags, 7
alcohol prices, 9
alerts, from professional organization, 68
American Public Health Association (APHA), 4, 68, 69, 87
approaches, skills and, 71–72
ask, importance of having in meeting with policymaker, 72
Association of State and Territorial Health Officials, 87
Austin, TX, earned sick leave policy of, 28

B

basic level, of engagement in policymaking, 67, 68, 78
de Beaumont Foundation, 39–40
Becker, J., 41
Benjamin, Georges, 4

Biden, Joe, 24, 45–46, 63
Big Cities Health Coalition, 87
bill, introduction of, 19
bipartisan support, for policies, 84
Black mothers, mortality rates of, 9
Bottoms, Keisha Lance, 18
Bowser, Muriel, 23
branches, of government, 17–18
Broockman, David, 45
budget
    of Congress, 21, *21*
    of government, 21, *21,* 90
business groups, challenging of Austin sick leave policies of, 28
business sector, influence on policy of, 71–72

C

Cairney, Paul, 44
Campaign for Tobacco Free Kids, 87
Center for Medicare and Medicaid Services (CMS), 69
Centers for Disease Control and Prevention (CDC), *20,* 32, 39–40
    backlash from Congress of, 2
    budgeting of, 21
    Federal health agency, 23, *25,* 32
    Health Impact in 5 Years (HI-5) initiative of, 9, 82
    Health in all policies resources, 90
    Stakeholder Engagement and Education, *11,* 11–13
    10 Essential Public Health Services, 12, *13*
Centers for Medicare and Medicaid Services (CMS), 34
Change Lab Solutions, 87
checks and balances, of US government, 18
chief executive officers (CEOs), 23
children, environmental justice and, 57
CityHealth, 40, 87–88
civil relationships, public health policy and, 84
Civil Rights Act, of 1990, 46
clear language, for policymaker meeting, 73
coalitions, 12, 52, 69
    and partnerships, 90
Coles, E., 36–37
collaboration, in policymaking process, 40–41, 81–85
comments to policymaker, suggestions for, 75–77
committee, for bill, 19
communities, policymaking and, 40–41
Community Catalyst, 69, 88

98 | POLICY ENGAGEMENT

community power, 40–41
Community Toolbox, 88
concise message for policymaker, importance of in meeting, 72
Congress
 CDC and, 2
 decision on budget of, 21
 role in ACA of, 18
Congress committees, different focuses of, 20
congressional appropriations process, 21
congressional districts, life expectancies across, 58
Constitution, of US, 26, 28, 37
context, for policymakers, 47–48, 48
coronavirus pandemic (COVID-19)
 CDC and, 2
 equity and, 55–56, 82
 eviction moratoriums and, 8
 minorities and, 9
 vaccine mandates and, 9
Council for Education on Public Health (CEPH), 3–4
Council Office of Racial Equity (CORE) of Washington, DC, 62
Council of the District of Columbia, 23
County Health Rankings and Roadmaps, 89
credentials of public health official, emphasis of, 76
credibility, emphasis on, 84, 85
cynicism, ineffectiveness in important meetings of, 73

D

Daniel, Katherine Lyon, 39
data
 amount to present, 47
 as state health agency activity, 27, 46
 insufficient, 63
decision-makers
 humanity of, 44–45
 identities of, 45
 motivations of, 45
 types of, 44
 understanding of, 43–44
decision-making process
 necessities to influence, 46–47, 47
 public health officials and, 7–14
Department of Health and Human Services (HHS), 21, 24, 25, 26, 32–33
 Public Health 3.0 initiative of, 60–61
Department of Health and Human Services Organizational Chart, 25
detail in oral testimony, written contrasted with, 74–75
detail in written testimony, oral contrasted with, 74–75
Diaz, Alicia, 24
Dickey Amendment, 20
Dingell, John, 22
direct lobbying, grassroots lobbying and, 38, 38–39
direct meetings, with policymakers, 77–78
dirt-park playground, testimony to Congress about, 39
District of Columbia (DC), metro card for children in, 55
Dobbs v. Jackson Women's Health Organization (court case), 28

donations, to organizations aligned with values of public health official, 70
drinking age, highway funding and, 21

E

Echt, Leandro, 48
editorials, writing of, 71
elected officials
 offer of advice to, 71
 relations with, 22
enactment, of policy, 8, 12, 14
environmental justice, children and, 57
equitable policies, 60–61
equity
 COVID-19 and, 55–56
 defined, 55
 equality contrasted with, 55
 geographic locations and, 56–57
 health, 57–63
 HIAs and, 61
 key concepts of, 56
evaluation, policy development and, 13–14
evidence, presenting to policymakers of, 46–47, 76
evidence-based policies, difficulties implementing of, 9, 10, 11
executive branch, of government, 17, 23–24
 role in ACA of, 18
Executive Order (13985), Advancing Racial Equity and Support for Underserved Communities, 63
executive signing, of bill, 19
extrinsic motivation, 45

F

fast-food workers in New York, unionization of, 45–46
Federal Advisory Committee Act (FACA), 70
federal agencies
 impact on public health of, 24–26, 25, 29
federal budget steps
 process of, 90
 timing and, 21
federal health agencies, 23–24
Federalist Papers (Hamilton), 26, 28
Federal Register, of agencies, 24
Federal Regulation of Lobbying Act, of 1946, 37
Fielding School of Public Health, of UCLA, 8
Fight for $15 movement, 45–46
Food and Drug Administration (FDA), 32–33, 75
Food and Nutrition Education in Schools Act, of 2021, 20
former regulators, influence on policy of, 70
Forrest, Katrina, 36, 95
Frey Evaluation, LLC, 71
full vote, on bill, 19
future potential health wins, 83

G

Geographic Insights, 57
geographic locations, equity and, 56–57

government
    branches of, 17–18
    budget process of, 21
    checks and balances of, 18
    executive branch of, 17, 18, 23–24
    judicial branch of, 18, 19, 26, 28
    legislative branch of, 17, 22–23, 29
    oversight role of legislative branch of, 22–23
    preemption, 18
    spending process of, 21–22
governmental policies, public health and, 7, 14, 17–18, 29
grassroots lobbying
    direct lobbying and, *38*, 38–39
    resources for, 90
gun violence research, restriction by Congress of, 20

H

Hamilton, Alexander, 26, 28
Harvard Center for Population and Development Studies, 57
Harvard Center of Geographic Analysis, 57
hazardous waste sites, in New Jersey, 39
health, adjudication of, 26, *27*, 28
health disparities, racist policies and, 8–9
health equity
    challenges to, 63
    policy change and, 57, 59, 63
    power and, 59–60
health impact assessments (HIAs), 60–61
    equity and, 62
Health Impact in 5 Years (HI-5) initiative, 9
Health Impact Project, 62
Health in all policies resources, 90
health inequities, plan for improving, 69
health law-making process, 20
health notes, 62
health policies, public health policies and, 3
Health Resources and Services Administration (HRSA), 32
health victories, of 21st century, *8*
hearings
    decision-maker motivation and, 46
    legislative oversight and, 22–23
    strategies for testifying at, 73–74
Hearne, Shelley, 39, 95
highway funding, setting of drinking age and, 21
Honest Leadership and Open Government Act, of 2007, 37
House Committee on Education and Labor, 20
House Committee on Energy and Commerce, 22
House of Representatives, passing of bill by, 19
Hughes, Charles Evan, 26
human service agencies, 33–34
humor, dangers of in important meetings, 73

I

identities, of decision-makers, 45
identity-based choices, 45

Indian Health Service (IHS), 33
inequity, roots causes of, 61–62, 63
Inseparable organization, 24, 88
interest groups, most common, 81–82
intermediate level, of policymaking engagement, 67, 68–69, 78
Internal Revenue Service, on lobbying, 37–38
intrinsic motivations, 46
issue, summary of, 78
Iton, Anthony B., 41, 91

J

Johns Hopkins Bloomberg School of Public Health, on policy engagement, 4, 90
judicial branch, of government, 18, 26, 28
    role in ACA of, 19
judicial review, 28

K

Kaiser Permanente, 40
Kemp, Brian, 18
Kingdon, John, 40–41
Kwiatkowski, Richard, 44

L

language
    adjustments trust of public and, 40
    in important meetings, 73
    in public comments audience and, 77
law-making process, 19
lead poisoning laws, 7
legislative body consideration, of bill, 19
legislative branch, of government, 17, 29
    oversight role of, 22–23
Legislative Health Notes, 90
Leifheit, Kathryn, 8
letters, to elected officials, 23
letters to the editor (LTEs), 71, 77, 78
levels of government, conflicts between, 18
life expectancy
    across congressional districts, *58*
    difference by block of, 56–57
lobbying, 36
    mistrust of public health profession of, 37–38
    resources for, 90
Lobbying Disclosure Act, of 1995, 37
local health departments, 26
local journalism, importance to local government of, 77

M

Markey, Edward, 68
mask mandates, in Georgia, 18
mass comments, precise public comments contrasted with, 75–76
Mayor's Order, on vaccinations, 23
media, policymaker influence of, 75–76

media advocacy, 91
meetings with policymakers
　clear language for, 73
　concise message in, 72
　cynicism in, 73
　personal reactions during, 72–73
　specific issue in, 72
　suggestions for, 71–73
mental health allies, leadership positions for, 24
mental health care policy, advocacy for, 24
message alignment, target audience with, 39–40, 41, 43
messiness, of policymaking, 35–36
methods, of policy engagement, 67–68
metro card, for children in District of Columbia (DC), 55
Michaels, David, 76
minimum tobacco age, attempted raising of, 35–36
mortality rates, of Black mothers, 9
most common interest groups, in policymaking, 81–82
motivation
　of decision-makers, 45–46
　extrinsic, 45
　intrinsic, 46
multi-sector collaboration, 41, 60

N

National Academies of Science (NAS), 1–2
National Association of City and County Health Officials, 88
National Center for Health Statistics, 56–57
National Center for Injury Prevention and Control, of CDC, 20
National Institutes of Health (NIH), 21–22, 25, 33
National Research Council, 61
National Rifle Association, 20
Needham, Massachusetts, 35–36
neighborhood public health policies, 7
Network for Public Health Law, 2, 88
New Jersey, hazardous waste sites in, 39
nonhealth policies, impact on health of, 7–11, *10*, 14
nonprofits, collaboration with state agencies of, 69–70, 81–82

O

Obama, Barack, 18, 20
Office of Management and Budget (OMB), of president, 21
opinion editorials (op-eds)
　as public voice, 71
　resources for, 91
　strategies for writing, 77
opposition, preparation for, 72–73, 76
oral testimony, written testimony contrasted with, 74–75
organizations aligned with values of public health official
　collaboration with, 81–82

donations to, 70
as starting point, 87–89
oversight role, of legislative branch of government, 22–23

P

partnerships, coalitions and, 90
Paul, Ilisa Halpern, 22
"People's Champion" title, 45
persistence, value of, 83
personal conviction of judges, law of land and, 28
personal reactions, while meeting with policymakers, 72–73
Pew Charitable Trusts, 61
Planned Parenthood v. Casey (court case), 28
Polan, Susan, 68
policy, landscape of, 17–29
policy advocacy organizations, volunteering with, 2, 70
policy analysis, problem identification and, 12
policy change
　equity and, 57, 58, 63
policy, defined, 7, 17
policy development, strategy and, 12
policy development component, of public health services, *13*
policy enactment, 12
policy implementation, 12–13
policymaker meeting, clear language for, 73
policymaker perceptions, political environment and, 1, 4
policymakers
　context for, 47–48, *48*
　direct meetings with, 77–78
　education of testifying of, 74
　evidence for, 46–47, 76
　familiarity with, 70–71
　necessities to influence, 46–47, *47*
　presenting of evidence to, 46–47
　relationship with, 74
　research skills and, 3, 4
　suggestions for meetings with, 71–73
　testifying before, 73–74
policymaking process
　best time to start, 11–12, 69
　collaboration in, 40–41, 69
　communities and, 40–41
　messiness of, 35–36, 41
　personal nature of, 36, 41
policy village, 81–82
politeness, during policymaker meetings, 72–73
political force, public health as, 2
political science models, for enacting government policies, 40–41
political system, public health officials and, 3, 63
political will, public health and, 1–2, 63
Porter, Keshia Pollack, 73, 95
power
　health equity and, 59–60
　shifting of, 60

precise public comments, mass comments contrasted with, 75–76
preemption, in government, 18
problem identification, policy analysis and, 12
professional organization, alerts from, 68
public comments, in agency rulemaking process, 75–77, 78
public health
  areas of greatest need for, 82, 85
  civil relationships and, 84
  distrust of public of term, 39–40
  emergence of, 2
  governmental policies and, 7, 14, 17–18, 29
  hearings and, 74
  impact of federal agencies on, 24–26, *25*, 29
  research and, 1
Public Health 3.0, 60
public health groups, alignment with values of public health official of, 69, 82
Public Health Needs Stronger Lobbying (Coles), 36–37
public health policies
  political engagement and, 2–3, 4, 82–85, *83*
  resources for, 90–91
  of US, 4

R

racial equity impact assessments (REIAs), 61–63
redlining, 8–9
registration, to vote, 68
representatives, awareness of, 68
research skills, policymakers and, 3, 4
Robert Wood Johnson Foundation, 62, 89
Roe v. Wade (court case), 28
roots causes, of inequity, 61–62, 63
rulemaking process, of agencies, 24–25, 75
rules, of government agencies, 24–26, *26*

S

section of proposal, focus on, 75
Senate, passing of bill by, 19
Senate Committee on Agriculture, Nutrition and Forestry, 20
skills, approaches and, 71–72
small wins, celebration of, 83
Smith, DB, 41
smoke-free laws, variability of, *10*
smoking bans, bars and, 9
Snyder, Harry M, 91
social change, policy change and, 55
social determinants or drivers of health (SDOH), 7–8, 57, 59
"solution," preference of public over term "policy," 40
Southerland, Betsy, 70
specific recommendation, importance of having for policymaker, 72, 76
spending process, of government, 20–22
staff of elected officials, respect for, 72, 78
stakeholder engagement, education and, *11*, 11–12, 14, 75

state agencies, collaboration with nonprofits of, 69–70
state health agency activities, range of, *27*, 87
state health departments, 26
state level legislation process, 19–20
State of Texas minimum wage law, business groups use of, 28
strategy, policy development and, 12, 14
structural racism, 59–60
subcommittee review, of bill, 19
Substance Abuse and Mental Health Services Administration (SAMHSA), 33
summary, of issue, 78
supermarkets, access to, 59
Supplemental Nutrition Assistance Program (SNAP), proposed reduced funding for, 61–62, 73
swimming pool analogy, 67
Swine Flu outbreak, of 1976, 2

T

Talking Health (de Beaumont Foundation), 39–40
target audience, message alignment with, 39–40, 41, 43
Ten Essential Public Health Services, 12, *13*
testifying, before policymakers, 73–74, 78
testimony, abbreviated, 75
Texas Court of Appeals, 28
Texas Supreme Court, 28
Tobacco 21 (T21) movement, 35–36
tobacco age raising, time spent for, 35–36
tobacco industry, extensive resources of, 35–36
tobacco restrictions, improvement of public health and, 9, *10*, 11, 35–36
tobacco taxes, 7
town halls, attendance of, 68
tribal governments, 17
Trust for America's Health, 89

U

unusual alliances, openness to, 84

V

vaccinations, Mayor's Order on, 23
values of public health official, organizations aligned with values of, 70
volunteering, with policy advocacy organizations, 70
voting, registration to, 68

W

Who Will Keep the Public Healthy? (National Academy of Medicine), 1–2
written testimony, oral contrasted with, 74–75

Z

Zimmermann, Alessandra, 90
zip code, differences in opportunity and, 57